INSIDER'S GUIDE TO REVERSE MORTGAGES

LEVERAGE THE APPRAISED VALUE OF YOUR HOME TO MAXIMIZE LIFE, INCOME, AND YOUR FULL BALANCE SHEET

JASON PARKER, MBA, CFP®, RICP®

An Insider's Guide to Reverse Mortgages
Leverage the Appraised Value of Your Home to Maximize Life, Income, and Your Full Balance Sheet

Print ISBN: 978-1-61206-276-1
eBook ISBN: 978-1-61206-277-8

Printed in the United States of America

CONTENTS

Introduction 5

1: What Is a Reverse Mortgage Anyway? 13

2: Is a Reverse Mortgage Right for You? 27

3: What Made Me Look at Reverse Mortgages? 39

4: Getting a Reverse Mortgage 59

5: The History of Reverse Mortgages 85

6: Common Questions About Reverse Mortgages 95

7: Creative Strategies to Maximize Your Retirement Using a Reverse Mortgage 111

8: A Quick Reference Guide to Reverse Mortgages 125

Conclusion 133

Acknowledgments 137

About the Author 139

Connect With Me 141

INTRODUCTION

When I first told colleagues I was going to step away from my financial planning job to write a book on reverse mortgages, you can imagine the looks on their faces. All of them hesitated before their well wishes, in a "bless your heart" kind of way, but I was prepared for that. I knew most wouldn't understand, but it didn't make it any less easy branching out alone, doing something close friends and family didn't seem comfortable with. I had done the academic and empirical research, so I was confident in the benefit of what I was doing, but it still seemed like a risk because I had almost no one else to talk to about it.

Those feelings were not much different than how people tend to feel when they're the first in their group of friends or family to get a reverse mortgage. Reverses mortgages still seem taboo, and very few people understand how they really work.

This book is not intended to make anyone a reverse mortgage expert, but it will teach you everything you need to know and consider before going any further in the process of getting a reverse mortgage. It will help those with existing reverse mortgages better explain the benefits to skeptical peers and help those looking to understand whether they should consider a reverse mortgage as an option in their financial planning. It will introduce concepts from the perspective of the end user, demonstrating how they impact real lives. You will better understand why reverse mortgages were created, how they were designed to increase quality of life, how they work, and things to look out for.

If you suddenly had access to more money, how would you improve your life?

What if you didn't have a mortgage payment to worry about month to month, or didn't have to worry about how you would pay your medical bills if something went wrong? What if your house would pay for it's own bills, such as property taxes, insurance, and repairs, like when the A/C unit or water heater needs to be replaced?

Maybe you've always wanted to travel more or have the time to spend with your grandkids. Maybe you've wanted to go fishing every weekend, collect classic cars, volunteer at an animal shelter, or be more involved in church activities. Or like many people, you dream of buying an RV and taking epic road trips across the continent without having to sell your house to cover the costs. It may be possible.

Unfortunately, many people are forced to work longer than they'd like for financial reasons, limiting the things they can do with their lives. If you've put off your hopes and dreams for years, waiting until you were done working to pursue your passions and live to the fullest only to discover you can't afford to do the things you've wanted to for so long, you've missed out on some of the best parts of life.

By living the retirement you've dreamed of, you can find new purpose in pursuing what matters most to you and staying active. It can even help you stay in better physical and mental shape to improve your health and longevity.

REVERSE MORTGAGE: THE RETIREMENT TOOL FEW PEOPLE ARE TALKING ABOUT THAT WILL CHANGE YOUR LIFE, IMMEDIATELY

You likely picked up this book because you or someone you love is considering a reverse mortgage. Maybe a friend or family member mentioned reverse mortgages to you, but you never discussed it with your financial advisor. Maybe you have never worked with a financial advisor or never knew who to ask about how they really work. Maybe you are house rich but feel like you're cash poor. Maybe you need to consolidate debt. Maybe you have a lot of investment assets, but you're worried about the volatility of the markets and selling low. Many financial advisors won't feel comfortable enough with reverse mortgages to recommend them, while those who do are often restricted by their companies from talking about them, not because they aren't safe or viable, but because the company worries that rogue advisors could cross-sell or recommend to put the proceeds into other products, where a big conflict of interest exists.

When I discovered the benefits reverse mortgages could have for many of my clients, I began to ask why they weren't being recommended more often. The reasons are twofold: First, reverse mortgages aren't included in the mandatory education for financial advisors, so many don't really know how they work or how they can best be used. Second, the possibility of an advisor incorrectly cross-selling proceeds from a reverse mortgage just to get a commission on another product isn't worth the risk for financial advisory firms that don't otherwise directly profit financially from reverse mortgages. While a reverse mortgage isn't a one-size-fits-all solution, it can be incredibly beneficial for many more people than have taken advantage of it.

In my various roles over decades of helping individuals of all ages with their finances and financial portfolios, I've heard themes from pre-retirees. People want to retire early enough to enjoy their freedom, and most want to have enough money in retirement that they don't have to work a part-time job just to pay their basic expenses. On the flipside, for actual retirees, I've heard a theme, "We see our total net worth and don't understand how we can feel like we are squeezing by each month." And more recently, "We've always thought we wanted to leave the house for the kids. But after living through the ups and downs over the years and then a pandemic, we've realized how short life can be. What can we do?"

Some advisors at that point will reply, "You need to cut your spending or you're going to run out of money," or "You have to think about selling your house," or "You can't afford to take less risk or inflation will run your portfolio into the ground, so there's nothing you can do but cut spending." But there is another way. In my opinion, it's a better way because you don't have to sacrifice any of your existing liquid assets. You can find money in your house.

Empowered by the introduction of housing wealth in financial and estate planning, I began looking at reverse mortgages as one of the best financial options on the market to help Americans use their full balance sheets, especially because the majority of seniors over 62 own their home. Homeownership for people ages 65 and older stands at over 75%[1].

1. Herbert, Christopher, and Jennifer H. Molinsky. "Homeownership Among Older Adults: A Source of Stability or Stress?" ASA Generations. Generations Journal, August 14, 2020. https://generations.asaging.org/homeownership-older-adults-stability-stress.

It's very likely reverse mortgages will be a huge part of the next iteration of holistic financial planning. We can't just rely on modern portfolio theory and stocks, bonds, and cash with the level of global inflation we're facing. Home equity is an often overlooked asset, though it's tightly intertwined with the U.S. financial system. And that is why evaluating a reverse mortgage is so valuable if you are 62 years old or older (55 in some cases). It might be the solution you are looking for to improve your financial status and allow you to live your retirement on your own terms.

In most things in life, you can't have your cake and eat it too. But, in this case, you can.

Reverse mortgages have answered the paradox. They're the silver bullet that offers a guarantee, security, and flexibility, freeing up cashflow by allowing you to live in your home while accessing its equity. They allow people to maximize life while they are alive and in many cases allow them to preserve higher return-generating liquid assets, giving them more flexibility later in life.

A reverse mortgage, in the simplest of terms, is the safe and responsible conversion of home equity into income tax-free money for retirees to use in any way they please. There's a cost to it, sure. What is that cost outside of upfront standard closing costs? It's the ongoing interest accumulating over time on any unpaid balance, despite the rate itself being lower than many other types of loans because of the quality of the collateral and the FHA insurance. That's it. No gotchas, no gimmicks, no hidden add-ons. The borrowers maintain full ownership and decision-making with the house, just like any traditional mortgage.

Reverse mortgages are one of the few ways a homeowner can tap into the equity they have in their home and convert it into purchase power for their daily life.

Another way to look at it is that the equity you currently have in your home from your years of work, planning, and luck can be spent the same as the dollar bills you have in your pocket. But that equity is a little more difficult to access than reaching into your pocket or purse to pull out cash.

The only way you can really access what your home is worth is either by selling it or by taking a loan out using the home as collateral, which you'd normally be required to start paying back right away, if you can even qualify for a loan as a retired person. For many, having to pay back the loan right away defeats the purpose of borrowing. It's not a viable solution. Once a forward loan is used, whether it's a home equity line of credit or cash-out refinance, if you ever miss a payment, you could be foreclosed on. The payments you make are mostly interest anyway, not even chipping away at principal until years later. That's part of the reason many people initially recoil at the notion of a reverse mortgage, because they think of how they'd never want a mortgage payment again and don't realize that is what makes reverse mortgages so special—there is no repayment until the last borrower leaves the house. That is also what makes it sound too good to be true. But it is a real option and many people who have done reverse mortgages love them.

Statistically, most people nearing retirement age own the home they live in, but there are many things that may come up in life that didn't allow for the house to be fully paid off. Once people reach retirement, their external earning capacity is limited for the rest of their lives. Unless someone chooses to continue to work, they're stuck drawing from the wealth they've accumulated up to that point. The home tends to be a large part of that wealth, but everyone still needs a place to live of course. So, they reach this paradox: how do they access a portion of the value they see in their home without jeopardizing the home itself or its future appreciation, while still living there? The reverse mortgage is the answer, by design.

The biggest benefit of a reverse mortgage is that it allows you to spend money you probably hadn't accounted for on whatever you want or need, as you need it.

Did you know that 65% of retirees' wealth is tied up in real estate? That means that the retired individuals in America right now are only living on 35% of what they have saved and accumulated over the years.

What would the lives of retirees in our country look like if they could tap into the other 65%? What would their quality of life look like? What would their healthcare look like?

Would they continue to work part-time? Or could they work until 62 and use their house to pay for those eight years while their social security base benefit accumulates instead?

A retired gentleman recently came to me along with his wife who is also retired. They have $800,000 in invested assets and a $500,000 property that they still owe $300,000 on. To make their budget work, even though he is technically retired and in his 70s, he still works a few days a week at the golf course. This is the solution they and their financial planner came up with to maintain the quality of life he and his wife had grown accustomed to over the years to avoid spending too deep into their savings. While they have other assets, their money is almost all in IRAs (Individual Retirement Accounts). Each dollar he pulls out of his traditional IRA is taxable. This plan works fine as long as his health holds up. Through a conversation with them and an appraisal estimate, I learned that they had equity in their house and planned to stay in the home for as long as they could afford to do so. They didn't understand the benefits of the hidden wealth in their home until they learned about reverse mortgages. All they saw ahead of them was the $1,600 payment every month for the next 20 years, so the house felt like a burden to maintain.

A reverse mortgage eliminated their monthly mortgage payment. While the couple still must pay property taxes and insurance, instead of their $1,600 monthly payment, their total housing cost is around $400 per month. Those savings allowed him to stop working and enjoy his retirement on his terms.

— 1 —

WHAT IS A REVERSE MORTGAGE ANYWAY?

A reverse mortgage is a one-of-a-kind cash loan from a bank, using your primary residence as collateral, which can be taken as a lump sum, an income stream for different periods of time, on an as-needed basis, or as a standby line of credit. The reason it is only available on a primary residence is because the lender knows you will take care of the house better if you live in it rather than renting it out. Remember the house is the only collateral, the only thing ever needed to repay the loan when you decide to permanently leave the home.

The simplest way for me to explain it is to compare it with the traditional mortgage, the mortgage you've likely known your whole adult life. With a traditional mortgage, you borrow money from the bank. You agree to make payments of principal and interest over the course of the next 15-30 years to pay that mortgage off. Most traditional mortgages are closed-end loans with a fixed term, so you know exactly how much you will pay above the sales price for the home before you even buy it. It typically ends up being hundreds of thousands in interest and yet people agree to pay that throughout their lifetimes, often without a flinch.

Your monthly payment on that mortgage likely includes a small portion for taxes and insurance and another small portion to pay down your principal, but for the first 10 years of the loan (the average loan length before selling or refinancing), a lot of what you pay each month goes toward interest.

A reverse mortgage is similar in that a bank still lends you money with your house as collateral—but you are not making monthly payments on the loan. You'll continue to pay your property taxes and insurance as you would whether you had a mortgage or not. Any money used from the reverse mortgage—the principal and any accrued interest—is due to be repaid either when the last borrower permanently leaves the home or if it falls into technical default due to delinquency on property charges. Also like any other mortgage, you can do whatever you'd like with the home, because you maintain ownership. A reverse mortgage is considered safer than a traditional mortgage because there is a reduced foreclosure risk with no monthly payment due.

The biggest difference between a traditional and reverse mortgage is the handling of the monthly interest on the loan balance. Interest still accrues as you use the money, but because you aren't making regular monthly payments, that interest is simply added to the balance of the loan. With a traditional mortgage, you have to make regular, mandatory, unforgivable payments. With a reverse mortgage, you don't have to make those payments, so your principal balance will gradually increase over time, until you leave the home and the loan becomes due. At that time, the loan is paid for by the remaining equity left in the home, with any shortfall backed by FHA. The house itself is the only collateral used to satisfy the balance, protecting all other personal assets.

As mentioned before, although you don't have a monthly mortgage payment, you are still responsible for any property expenses (property taxes, homeowners insurance, HOA fees, upkeep, and utility charges based on square footage) just like you are with a traditional mortgage. Remember, even though you don't have to make a payment toward the reverse mortgage balance, there is no prepayment penalty so you *can* make elective payments. When you make a payment on a reverse mortgage, it does the same thing as when you make a payment on a traditional mortgage—your unpaid balance goes down.

There are two primary types of reverse mortgages: private and government-insured. While there are certainly instances when a private reverse mortgage is the way to go, in most situations, the government-insured option should be considered first. Government-insured reverse mortgages are better known as home equity conversion mortgages, or HECMs (pronounced "heck-ums").

Many people ask, "What happens if my home becomes worth less than it is now, or what if the balance grows so big it's greater than the market value?" HECMs (home equity conversion mortgages), which are HUD-designed reverse mortgages, are insured by the FHA. If we should go through another housing crisis or you outlive the actuary table and you pass away with a higher loan balance than the home is worth, the FHA mortgage insurance covers you. That's why the lender offers this type of loan with such a good rate, as compared to other reverse mortgage options without insurance that come at a higher rate. For many reverse mortgage borrowers, a HECM is the best option.

FHA-insured HECMs account for over 90% of all reverse mortgages today. The other 10% of reverse mortgages are called "proprietary" and are typically used for jumbo loan situations to maximize money available, certain situations where borrowers may not want to pay the mortgage insurance upfront because of a shorter term, or other unique situations. Proprietary reverse mortgages may have special provisions and can sometimes offer higher payout rates. They're more often available on higher valued homes with loans up to $4 million while still being non-recourse like the HECM.

Non-recourse means the bank has no legal right to go after anything or anyone other than the house for any accrued balance, regardless of what happens to the housing market after getting the loan. Part of what you get from the FHA insurance is transferring the risk of a decrease in value or outliving the actuary table they use to determine how much you can borrow at certain ages. Even with a loss, the bank cannot go to you, your children, or your estate to demand payment. Instead, the mortgage insurance from FHA covers those losses on HECMS, and proprietary reverse mortgages are written off above what was garnered from the home sale.

According to a study done by the nonprofit Urban.com, somewhere around 80-90% of people have an intent around the age of retirement (age 70) to pass on their house to their kids. However, only around 50% still live in that home when they reach 80. Most people end up selling the home in their 80s due to a spouse passing or a need for assisted living. In their 70s, they lack the foresight to plan for all possible outcomes, but by waiting until frailty and aging sets in, the options can become much more limited and traumatic. They make decisions based on an ideal of thinking they'll stay in the home indefinitely, that isn't, statistically speaking, always a possibility once the effects of aging set in.

REVERSE MORTGAGE REQUIREMENTS

There are a few baseline requirements to be eligible for a reverse mortgage: **age**, **equity**, and **primary residence status**. A borrower must be 62 or older to qualify for a HECM, although some states, such as Arizona, allow proprietary jumbo reverse mortgages as young as 55.

There are three factors that determine how much someone has access to: youngest borrower's age, appraised value at the time of the loan, and future projected interest rates. Like all reverse mortgages, the percentage you can borrow will be lower the younger the borrower and a higher percentage the older you are. On HECMs *only*, eligible non-borrowing spouses (NBS) are fully protected below borrowing age, but because they retain the legal right to remain in the home even once the borrower has passed away (meaning the lender has to wait even longer to be repaid), the amount eligible to be borrowed is based on that younger, non-borrowing spouse.

The other main requirement is you must have enough equity in your home to use based on the factors mentioned above. For HECMS, the FHA uses a life expectancy table to estimate statistically how long you are likely to live in your home before the lender would ever get repaid. The future projected interest rate is used in case borrowers keep the mortgage long-term. So the FHA publishes the base amount you can borrow based off the 10-year treasury rate, even though the actual charged rate is based on the shorter-term one-year treasury rate (one-year CMT).

A younger borrower may have access to approximately 40% (up to $160,000 on a $400,000 valued home) of the appraised value, whereas someone in their 80s could have up to 60% (up to $240,000 on a $400,000 valued home). In either case, ample equity is retained in the property by design.

It is important to remember that the starting loan limit based on all the factors above, called the principal limit, needs to be applied to any existing liens first, possibly reducing actual cash received. But even in that case, the borrower still receives the same present-value economic benefit, without having to make the monthly payments anymore on the extinguished mortgage, adding up to tens of thousands a year in freed-up cashflow, a reduction in daily stress, and increased happiness, which is hard to put a number on.

Here's a hypothetical example: A 62-year-old borrower has up to $160,000 available to borrow on a $400,000 valued home. They owe $100,000 on their forward mortgage with monthly payments due of approximately $1,800. They really want it paid off so they can retire, so they are paying an extra $500 per month towards it without sacrificing other savings. It has been very stressful because they are working more and don't have the energy to do all the things they want on the weekend. They have done everything right, saved well, and will be ready to retire once the monthly payment goes away. With a reverse mortgage, they would have $160,000 available they could use to pay off the existing lien/mortgage of $100,000, leaving an additional $60,000 in a line of credit for later or to supplement or delay social security. They live a healthy lifestyle and plan on longevity but never wanted to work past 62. Now using the home equity, they have many different options to retire right now, guilt free, and maximize their balance sheets, existing assets, and happiness. They didn't have $160,000 to spend, because $100,000 had to pay off the existing mortgage. If the house had no mortgage and was completely paid off, then the full $160,000 would be available to the borrower after a year. (Cash withdraws are generally limited to 60% the first year with the remaining 40% available thereafter.)

Finally, for all reverse mortgages, it's a legal requirement that you live in the home, and it must be your primary residence. The primary residency requirement does not preclude the borrower(s) from owning other homes, one borrower to be in rehab for an extended time, or even from using proceeds of a reverse mortgage to pay cash for an income property or family vacation home. All lenders require borrowers to maintain the property that has the reverse mortgage lien. In a sense that's how lenders keep borrowers' skin in the game, but it's not overly restrictive—it's common sense. Owner-occupiers tend to maintain their property better than a tenant or renter, and in some cases property values are ruined by renters or vacancy, which is what the lenders, investors, and even taxpayers want to avoid.

Besides age and equity qualifications, it's important for borrowers to consider what setting they want to live in long-term. Is staying in your home even your objective? Remember you must maintain the ability to pay property taxes and homeowner's insurance while you remain in and care for that home.

The only borrower financial underwriting that is done for a reverse mortgage is verification that borrowers can at least afford minimum property charges. That is a safety net that was added as an enhancement in the wake of the 2008 financial crisis where many property owners with reverse mortgages lost homes due to not paying property taxes or other property charges. It unfairly gave the product a bad reputation as it had nothing to do with the reverse mortgage itself, but property owners had not been screened to make sure they had any other assets to even pay the property taxes. And when many people lost savings and jobs or spent all the equity at once, they did not have the income to pay property taxes, pay insurance, or maintain the home. Most borrowers qualify for this financial requirement based on showing social security income statements alone. But a good loan officer will have a few other ways to safely ensure borrowers qualify with income if possible. It is all in the spirit of protecting borrowers long-term and is technically called the Financial Assessment, which ensures there is a minimum level of residual income even after accounting for those obligations.

A Note on Private Reverse Mortgages

The most common type of non-government insured reverse mortgage is a called a proprietary or private loan. They are a relatively newer market that is rapidly expanding to fill the gaps in the market where HECMs may not be a good fit but homeowners want access to some of their home equity while still living in the house. They are mostly jumbo loans, meaning an amount larger than the government loan limit, which is $970,800 in 2022. These loans can apply to homes valued at $8,000,000 or more.

Each year, the FHA releases the nationwide loan limits in an annual bulletin. It's all public information and can be found by Google searching for "FHA HECM mortgagee letters." To find every detail of the FHA reverse mortgage program, read the **Administration of Insured Home Mortgages Handbook (4330.1)** at https://www.hud.gov/program_offices/administration/hudclips/handbooks/hsgh/4330.1

Currently, the limit is $970,800. So, a home could be worth $2 million and completely paid off, but if someone were to use that home to do a government-insured reverse mortgage, the loan amount would be limited to that maximum dollar amount set by the FHA based on the age of the youngest borrow, which may be only $400,000. For a loan that exceeded that maximum, you would need to secure a private reverse mortgage, and could potentially get access for up to $1,200,000 on the same house, a $800,000 increase. That amount could buy an entire property for cash, so the access to an increased amount is very important for certain types of buyers who use the loan proceeds for real estate or other big ticket expenditures.

Remember, proprietary reverse mortgages aren't insured by the government so they have a higher interest rate to offset the risk, sometimes have minimum borrowing amounts initially, and do not have the same protections for non-borrowing spouses. The good thing is that most proprietary mortgages are designed very similarly to their HECM cousins with safety provisions and they should all be non-recourse as well.

Lastly, proprietary loans are typically underwritten by the major companies in the industry but can be offered by anyone affiliated with them as a loan officer or broker. Like always, make sure you are working with someone who can tell you their affiliation with companies other than just themselves, and whether it is a broker relationship where they are a middleperson (which is okay) or principal agent (which can sometimes give more flexibility).

From a math standpoint, a reverse mortgage is a negative amortization loan—another phrase that makes people recoil who heard the horror stories of 2008 and the wild west of lending that led to the loss of so many homes. Those negative amortizing loans were much different and included being recast to higher rates or required balloon payments at a future date, often way beyond the borrower's capacity. People gambled that they'd flip the home before payments were required, banks turned a blind eye, and once the downturn hit, it was a disaster.

Reverse mortgages are not that type of loan in any way other than the interest accumulation. In traditional or forward mortgages, the amortization table starts with the amount you borrowed, with all the interest calculated, frontloading a large portion of it, and amortizes it down into monthly payments so that by the end of the mortgage term you owe zero and then the lien is removed.

TRADITIONAL MORTGAGE EXAMPLE

Loan amount	$200,000.00
Term	30 years
Interest rate	4%
Monthly payment (PI)	$954.83
Total principle and interest payments	$343,739.43
Total interest	$143,739.43

A reverse mortgage is the reverse of that. You begin with a borrowed amount, but instead of the balance going down to zero, the interest is added to the loan balance each month, at a fixed or variable rate. The borrower doesn't have to pay any of the balance back until the last borrow leaves the home. In strong housing markets, it's not uncommon for people to have reverse mortgages for only a few years, see rapid appreciation on their home without ever having made a payment, and sell for a profit with no cashflow out. People may move multiple times in retirement, using a reverse mortgage on each home they buy to free up other liquid assets.

REVERSE MORTGAGE EXAMPLE (LUMP SUM)

Lump sum advance	$200,000.00
Years	30
Monthly loan payment	$0.00 per month
Interest rate	4%
Total payments you will have received	$200,000.00
Total interest accumulated	$462,699.71*
Ending mortgage balance	$662,299.71*

**paid by house*

There's a common phrase many in the industry say when describing the flexible nature of the decision on a reverse mortgage: "It's just a mortgage." A reverse mortgage is simply a lien on the home for a balance due. No mortgage payment is ever due and the interest is allowed to accumulate on the balance, which is what negative amortization means. Even if the balance of the loan becomes greater than the value of the home, the FHA is responsible to pay the lender the difference. That is why there are now updated limits on borrowing by FHA and private lenders to minimize the likelihood that no equity will remain, though the borrower is protected credit-wise if it happens.

A reverse mortgage eventually becomes due when the last borrower leaves the home permanently, whether through selling the home, moving to another residence, or passing away. At that point, the lien must be paid off, usually through the sale of the home. The estate and heirs have options though, just like they would if the owners died with a forward mortgage remaining. In fact, they may have more time to decide what they want to do in the case of a reverse mortgage.

One of the best aspects of reverse mortgages are the many creative ways they can be structured to fit your goals using full balance sheet planning. You could set up an unused future line of credit that increases over time, or use a reverse mortgage to pay off an existing mortgage. Or you may use it to gain access to cash to spend or give away to family or charity so you can appreciate your wealth while you're alive. Whatever the goal, HECMs and other reverse mortgages allow homeowners to tap into their home's equity without crunching cashflow or risking a missed mortgage payment.

REVERSE MORTGAGES IN REAL LIFE

Isabel Medina, a widow, lived in Southern California. Her kids lived a couple hours away from her. She lived in the house that she and her husband paid off. It was their plan to live out the rest of their retirement in this home. Unfortunately, Isabel's husband, Isaac, suffered a heart attack two years ago. The last couple of years, Isabel lived alone in the home, far enough from her children that she didn't get to see them as often as she'd like. She was desperate to move closer to them.

While Isabel had some assets and income, she had other financial worries that kept her from making the move. What if her house wouldn't sell? What if it did, but it didn't give her enough to cover a new home near her kids and she'd be left with a mortgage payment?

Paralyzed by these fears, Isabel lived in the house, miserable, for two years. She felt trapped. She didn't know there was another way.

Then she learned about reverse mortgages. She sold her home, allowing her to remedy the immediate pain point—she didn't want to live there anymore. Selling allowed her to take the equity out. Next, she used a reverse mortgage to purchase her new $600,000 home just a few blocks from one of her children.

Her original home sold for $600,000, and she netted $500,000. She put $300,000 down on the new home, but because she used a reverse mortgage—a HECM for purchase—she will never have a mortgage payment. This allowed her to keep that additional $200,000 for emergencies or to use however she wants.

Isabel was able to sell her house, which closed the door on that chapter of her life and helped heal some of the emotional scars of being there. But the benefits expanded to her children as well. Because she was able to move closer to them, she's now able to provide free childcare for her grandchildren. This has helped her kids pursue new career opportunities and saved them money in daycare costs.

Now Isabel is feeling more fulfilled and is blossoming in her new role as a hands-on grandparent. She's also less anxious because she knows she has some excess money set aside. All it took was finding the wealth in her house.

— 2 —

IS A REVERSE MORTGAGE RIGHT FOR YOU?

When considering someone's interest in reverse mortgages, I tend to look at the bigger picture first. To be able to give the most objective and professional opinion, I need to understand things from the borrower's perspective and learn what made them consider a reverse mortgage as an option.

- What triggered their interest?
- What's their motivation, and what changed in their situation to now look for alternatives?

From there it becomes much clearer where the priorities are and what needs to be diagnosed.

- What are the pros and cons?
- Who is impacted by the decision and what are the contingencies?
- What other assets are available and how are they being applied?
- What are all the possible income sources and how sustainable or desirable is each?
- For investment-minded borrowers: do they like where they live and think where they live is a good investment using the same logic they considered when they bought the home?

While I don't generally advocate most people use leverage to buy real estate solely as an investment, especially when it involves your primary residence and sanctuary, it would be naïve to think that people don't consider resale value when they are looking at where to buy a home. So it's still prudent to at least factor in future appreciation and desirability when considering a reverse mortgage.

Before reading through the chapters in this book, I encourage you to ask those same questions of yourself:

- What triggered my interest in reverse mortgages?
- What changed in my life that motivated me to explore reverse mortgages as an option?
- Why is my initial reaction that reverse mortgages are a bad thing? What made me feel that way? Where did I read something negative, or who said it? Did I look into what actually happened or read deep enough to consider the story?

This will help you keep your underlying goals in mind as we walk through the mechanics of this retirement drawdown tool and common use scenarios as well as busting some myths.

Beyond understanding someone's reasons for looking into reverse mortgages, I want to dig even deeper to get to the why behind the why. For me it is important to see both objectively as a professional third party and through the client's eyes, with any emotions accounted for and discussed.

Usually, their reasons will fall under one of three primary goals:

1. They want to get access to money as they please out of an existing, fully paid off property.
2. They have an existing mortgage, home equity line of credit, or some other lien that they're making mandatory monthly payments toward, and they no longer want to deal with

those recurring payments, or they want mitigate any risk of foreclosure, a credit hit, or losing the home if something were to happen health-wise or the market downturned and they missed a payment.

3. They want to have access to the equity to use it as part of a strategic financial plan in coordination with other assets for income tax strategies or potentially buying a second home for themselves or for family.

We'll dig into all three of these goals more, but I want to take a second to explain what I mean by that third goal. Strategic use of the equity is where the biggest untapped opportunity lies for most people.

The money that comes out of the reverse mortgage line of credit is income tax-free.*

(*This is not tax advice. Consult a tax advisor if you have concerns.)

To get the maximum flexibility, a lot of people will use an adjustable rate structure to gain access to a line of credit. They will do this as early as they can in retirement to get it set up before they need it. That way the line of credit has been established and has grown by the time they eventually need it later on, maybe to supplement an income stream, fund in-home long-term care, update the house, or remodel for aging by putting in ramps and railings or increasing automated features.

Unlike many traditional HELOCs from commercial banks, the HECM reverse mortgage line of credit can never be frozen, reduced, or canceled as long as its simple rules are followed. That is very reassuring to many retirees who need to know it will be there when they really need it, regardless of external economic conditions. Any unused balance on the HECM line of credit can grow at the interest rate of the loan, regardless of whether property values drop or rise. (Proprietary reverse mortgage lines of credit are similar in many ways, but the line of credit growth may be calculated differently and capped in some cases, so make sure to work with a reputable lender.)

Whether a reverse mortgage is right for you depends on a great number of factors that are hard to cover in a book. Over the following chapters, I hope to give you a strong understanding of how reverse mortgages work and the ways that you can strategically use them to maximize your retirement. However, there is no substitute for professional guidance. Think of this book as the first stepping stone, and if you think a reverse mortgage might be right for you, reach out to a financial planner or qualified financial advisor who understands reverse mortgages well to help you determine how to reach your retirement goals.

REVERSE MORTGAGE MISCONCEPTIONS

Because of a lack of reverse mortgage education amongst financial professionals, there are many misconceptions. These are the three I hear most often:

1. "It sounds too good to be true."
2. "It's a last resort and I'm not there yet."
3. "I'll end up losing my house."

So, let's clear those up right away. It's not too good to be true. It doesn't have to be a last resort. And if you are a financially responsible person, it is unlikely you'll end up losing your house.

Reverse mortgages were designed exclusively for seniors to give them a viable option for maximizing their choices in their golden years. Over time, more and more protections have been implemented to make this process safer than ever. Let's bust some myths!

Misconception #1: "It's just like having another mortgage and I'll be paying another monthly payment."

All FHA loans follow the same basic guidelines and are standardized loans, so a reverse mortgage is no different than FHA conventional mortgages in that way. However, no monthly mortgage payments are required as long as you meet the terms of the loan. You must continue to pay your property taxes, homeowner's insurance, HOA fees, and home maintenance costs, the same as you would with a forward mortgage. If you would like to make payments (monthly or otherwise) to reduce the loan balance, you can.

Here are some other differences between a reverse and forward mortgage:

- Reverse mortgages do not require a FICO score minimum.
- The loan balance of a reverse mortgage increases over time, while a forward mortgage loan balance decreases.
- With a reverse mortgage, the borrower can select from a variety of payout options.
- A forward mortgage includes a set term for the end of the loan. A reverse mortgage loan is paid when a maturity event occurs.
- A reverse mortgage is a non-recourse loan.

Misconception #2: "I won't be protected if my loan balance exceeds the value of my home."

This scenario is exactly why FHA mortgage insurance exists. FHA mortgage insurance is put in place because the lenders don't want to be on the hook if there's a loss due to decreased property values or if a loan balance exceeds home values due to longevity. This leaves you as the borrower with significant peace of mind over the years you may have one, and it also gives a sense of security to your heirs.

This insurance is also part of what allows this loan to be non-recourse, which is one of the key differences between reverse and forward mortgages.

Non-Recourse Loans

A non-recourse loan, in this instance, means the following:

- The home is the only asset that can be used to pay off the loan. The lender only gets repaid from the proceeds of the property sale.
- Your heirs won't inherit any debt unless they choose to. In fact, they receive any proceeds from the property sale if there are any remaining after repayment.
- Borrowers can never owe more than the appraised value of the home at the time the loan is due. If your loan balance is higher than your home's value, your heirs aren't liable for paying the difference (unless they were already living in the home).

Mortgage Insurance Premium

By paying the mortgage insurance premium (MIP), you gain the protections listed above. Your MIP is charged at closing (upfront MIP) and added each month to your loan balance (monthly MIP).

The upfront MIP is a one-time fee and equals 2% of your maximum claim amount.

The monthly MIP is charged each month and is figured by multiplying your loan balance by 0.5% and dividing that out across 12 months. FHA has made several changes over the years to the formula as the market evolves to minimize the likelihood taxpayers would have to burden any cost.

Misconception #3: "Reverse mortgages are a last resort."

It's true that currently reverse mortgages are still most often used as a last resort, but that doesn't mean they should be. Unfortunately, it's simply due to inertia, meaning many people don't take action until they're forced to.

Statistically speaking, the point of desperation really is the worst time to do a reverse mortgage. Whatever behaviors resulted in a desperate financial situation to begin with probably haven't changed overnight now that a person has access to more money, so it's worth looking at all options available at that point. What are they going to do with that money now that they have more?

However, when carefully considered as part of an overall financial plan, reverse mortgages can be a flexible tool for retirement. You can choose to receive the proceeds as a lump sum, in predetermined payments, as a line of credit, or even in a combination. There are benefits to setting up a reverse mortgage long before a last resort scenario. Reverse mortgages can be a valuable part of a plan for seniors looking to unlock financial freedom in retirement. The sooner the better for many.

Misconception #4: "There are a lot of defaults on these types of loans."

The FHA implemented their mandatory independent HECM counseling to mitigate these very concerns at the inception of the program back in 1988. They want to ensure you can meet the financial obligations of the loan. They even created the option for life expectancy set asides (LESAs) so money can be set aside from the loan proceeds to pay taxes and insurance.

The most common reason for defaults on reverse mortgages is borrowers not paying their property taxes. But even if you didn't have any kind of mortgage and you didn't pay your property taxes, the county would foreclose on your property. It has nothing to do with the reverse mortgage itself. After the Financial Crisis of 2008, Congress audited reverse mortgage counseling sessions and discovered borrowers may not have been given all the information they needed to understand ongoing property obligations.

The new, stricter financial assessment rules requiring lenders to underwrite the borrowers for their property charges, set up in 2014, drastically reduced tax and insurance defaults. This is a great safeguard to make sure borrowers have the ability to meet these obligations.

As long as you do these three things, you won't default:

1. Maintain the home as your primary residence
2. Stay current on your property taxes, insurance, HOA fees, and any mandatory property charges like assessments

3. Perform any necessary maintenance and upkeep to the home to avoid collateral deterioration

It's not like a forward mortgage where you could get behind on mortgage payments, leading to a default on the loan.

Misconception #5: "I'll be paying way too much in interest."

Let's look at some numbers. Let's say you have an $800,000 home and you do a reverse mortgage for $400,000. Regardless of the reverse mortgage, your home is still worth $800,000 and you're keeping 100% of any net appreciation on the house.

The only thing that is accruing interest is that $400,000.

Suppose your interest rate is 4%. After year one, your balance is going to be about $416,000. Your home value is still $800,000.

Two years later, you're looking at a loan balance of around $432k. Three years later, $450k. At the same time, your house has likely gone up significantly in value. And remember, if you sell your home, your loan balance is just paid off at closing.

Compare these interest payments to a forward mortgage. If you bought a $300,000 home with a forward mortgage and paid it off over a 30-year period, you probably paid somewhere over $500,000 in interest our of pocket! However, we are conditioned to find regular mortgage interest payments as simply the cost of owning a home.

Misconception #6: "The word 'reverse' means you're losing all the forward progress you've made on your regular mortgage."

It's important to understand that a mortgage, whether forward or reverse, is just a legal instrument that pledges a house as collateral for a loan. In financial terms, it's called leverage. That's it.

The word "reverse" is included in the name to indicate that the payment stream is reversed. Instead of you paying money to the bank, the bank pays money to you.

The house is responsible for its own loan at all times, backed by the FHA insurance embedded in the product. Sometimes I'll hear people interpret "reverse" as "go back on" when that's not necessarily true.

First Position Lien

If you have multiple liens, the reverse mortgage must be in first position. Basically, this means that your reverse mortgage lender has first dibs on any collateral value over any other liens, like a solar lease. They're first in line as a creditor to the value of the home. Any mortgage liens need to be extinguished too. So, if you had $50,000 left on your mortgage and also had a $10,000 HELOC that was tapped for a couple of thousand, those amounts must be paid off with your reverse mortgage loan.

Misconception #7: "This product isn't for high-net-worth individuals."

Many people think a reverse mortgage is only for those who are struggling with money. This couldn't be further from the truth. The leak of the Panama Papers in 2016 gave us a window into the tax strategies of billionaires, while many advisors to high income, high net-worth clients already knew this. What do they do? They have a stock portfolio or other assets that they borrow against, and they live within that borrowed money. It is income tax-free money. Then they make enough money on what they borrow doing other things.

For high-net-worth individuals, reverse mortgages are not about financial need. They are about finding cash flow options that are tax efficient and strategically using leverage within the rules of the law. Besides the benefit of not creating an additional monthly payment, a reverse mortgage allows you to access home equity without much tax impact and without selling investment portfolios that may be appreciating.

The income tax-free loan proceeds one can access from a reverse mortgage actually makes this product a very appealing prospect for higher-net-worth, portfolio-minded individuals.

No matter your net worth, why would you leave $800,000 of cash just sitting in old mortar and bricks and drywall? It doesn't make sense if you can use it for other things.

Misconception #8: "Isn't this a scam?"

As with anything that has to do with money, scams exist. But those scams are not the product itself. The HECM or reverse mortgage is not the problem. Human beings who will try to manipulate you are the problem. I've often heard the way they are usually advertised on infomercials adds to the scam feeling.

Reverse mortgage "scams" can take many forms, including impersonating a licensed loan officer or lender. Or someone may try to talk you into doing the loan for an outcome that isn't in your best benefit. An example could be if someone came to you with an investment opportunity and told you it had a $100,000 buy in, but you would stand to make a million. When you tell them you don't have that $100,000 to give them, they might say, "Oh, you don't? Well, you have equity in your home, don't you? You could do a reverse mortgage to get that amount!"

Whatever the case may be, you have to go on high alert when other people start trying to get access to your money by any means. The vehicle they've chosen may just happen to be a reverse mortgage. This is another reason why it is so important to have that third-party counseling and why you should be as honest as possible with everyone you consult with (HUD counselor, advisor, and loan officer) about the reasoning behind your decisions. They are there to help you make a more informed decision about whether a reverse mortgage is the right product for your specific needs.

Peace of Mind

When you do a reverse mortgage, the equity you can access is limited. This is a mathematical protection that ensures there is ample equity to offset projected future interest if it accrues. It benefits not only the homeowner to have more flexibility as time goes on, but also the lender to be able to get repaid at some point in the future. No matter the reason, all reverse mortgages are legally non-recourse loans, meaning no borrower nor their heirs are liable for repaying the loan. The house can still be passed down to children if that's something the borrower wants to do. I always recommend working with a knowledgeable financial planner who can run through full-picture financial scenarios with you.

— 3 —

WHAT MADE ME LOOK AT REVERSE MORTGAGES?

If financial advisors aren't talking about reverse mortgages, what made me start exploring them more thoroughly in previous roles? I got into this industry to help people and from the beginning I knew I would need to learn all the rules of the game to be successful.

For me, it all began after an unfulfilling first quarter in college and joining the Army Reserve. I bought into everything it stood for, phrases like "Integrity is what you do when no one is watching," and "Do the right thing because it's the right thing to do." I was fortunate to get a special operations job, go to foreign language school, and learn the mostly useless but exciting skill of jumping out of airplanes. As my six-year Army contract was ending, I was eager to join the workforce as I had already interned at two major Wall Street firms as a college student.

But just a month before the end of my Army contract, stop-loss was activated for the first time since Vietnam. My service was extended. I was mobilized in January of 2003 to Fort Bragg, and then I was deployed to Iraq in April of that year. At first, we expected to be on the ground just a couple of months because we were Reservists, but I wouldn't return home until April 2004. I still had two quarters of college left.

After completing my degree at Ohio State, I made the long one-way drive from Columbus, Ohio, to Scottsdale, Arizona. I got my first real job out of school at Morgan Stanley, where I completed their licensing and training program. I treated my first couple years in the industry like a medical student's residency: I wanted to learn as many aspects of the industry that weren't taught in textbooks as I could to be more well-rounded as I found my ultimate niche. Those years served me well for the rest of my career as I learned how things fit together behind the scenes in the industry, outside of each company's own silo.

Eventually I moved to a financial advisor position at a large financial services company in Phoenix. This was where I found a home. I was able to do a high volume of real life financial planning and talk to clients all day without having to spend any time marketing. While in that role, it was the Certified Wealth Strategist (CWS®) curriculum by Cannon Financial Institute that turned me on to more complex financial planning beyond just varieties of stocks and bonds, and the small reference to reverse mortgages was my first exposure to the concept. I learned about full balance sheet financial planning—literally looking at every resource available, just like you would for a business. I learned all the strategies used by the wealthy with trusts, investments, liability, taxes, estate, charitable giving, and wealth transfer.

I had started as a call center-based national advisor and moved up quickly to a wealth manager role. As the company began to expand their face-to-face offerings, they asked if I would help open a San Diego office. That was a great honor in my career, not only helping get that office off the ground, but establishing deep personal relationships with retired clients in a face-to-face setting.

In that position, I had many clients who were veterans or retired federal employees. They all had pensions and good work-life balance throughout their careers, had accumulated decent savings, and were seemingly happier in retirement. Contrasting their demeanor and situations with wealthy clients who had been executives and were often more stressed out really stuck with me. I saw how the balance between income and assets, guarantees versus market risk, all played out in people's lives and the decisions they made.

GETTING GOOD FINANCIAL ADVICE

Through my various jobs within this industry, I have seen that there is sadly no true measure for quality of advice. While this is an issue I believe industry regulators at every level can and should address, for now it's up to the consumer to determine whether the advice they are receiving is good or not. (And who they should listen to when everyone seems to call themselves an advisor.)

A financial advisor you connect with and who does exactly what you need is worth the effort to find. Some advisors display emotion, some don't. Some like more teaching and coaching, others just do trading. Some advisors can be all those things! But all too often consumers will pick the first advisor on their list or choose based on a brand name. The advisor's background in a client's circumstances matters. If you don't get a good fit on your first try, don't be afraid to keep looking.

Once my son was born, I too wanted to try the work-life balance I saw so many past clients enjoy, so I took a federal job offered in Nashville, Tennessee. There, I worked for veterans within the VA pension and disability system and also worked directly with the VA home loan program as an underwriter and lender auditor. It was at this job that I saw the inside of a government insured program.

I eventually transitioned back into the industry at a well-known investment management company in Arizona where I worked with high-net-worth clients as a financial planner and manager of financial advisors.

Now I've transitioned my career to specializing solely in home equity planning and reverse mortgages based on the need for quality education I've seen firsthand.

The theme throughout my career journey has been about looking for better ways to help people.

I've never been okay with the status quo in the financial advice industry, and I want to make a difference. I've been driven and motivated by doing the right thing. As a lifelong consumer financial advocate, I feel honored to have worked with thousands of past clients at the intersection of money, emotions, life, and mortality.

HOUSING IS WHO WE ARE

Before transitioning to focus fully on the use of home equity in retirement, my quest to improve my value and industry education eventually led me down the rabbit hole to better understanding housing in financial planning and retirement. I found so many of my conversations with clients centered around their real estate and housing plans, where their kids and grandkids live, long-term care considerations, housing contingency planning, and how home equity was burning a hole in their pocket. Yet there is very little industry training on these topics for advisors.

As academic articles about housing assets began to get sprinkled into publications like the Financial Planning Journal, I started to apply what I learned to my own clients. I initiated those conversations, and I could see the apprehension and anxiety of my clients drop considerably when we went deeper, talking about their housing plans. Why? Because it was something they were comfortable talking about.

As conversations got deeper, one thing became painfully clear: housing is a huge part of who we are as people. Where we live matters. The houses we own matter. What they look like matters. It's having the space and square footage we are used to. It's the garage we either love or hate but are nonetheless grateful for. It's the landscaping all our neighbors know us for. These little things mean a lot to us. To ignore that entire dynamic, like much of the investment world does, is missing one of the primary drivers of client motivation as they move through life.

When I'd ask prospective clients a question about their investments, they could get cagey, give a canned answer, or get defensive. They were unsure of themselves because they were unsure of the "right" answer, and they didn't want to sound naïve. When I'd ask what their "plans" or "goals" were, they would often clam up and look at each other, not sure how to answer. But when I asked about their house or housing plans, they would light up and spill every detail of an actual plan that covered the next 15 years or more of their lives. We're knowledgeable about our homes because our homes are part of our identities.

In my opinion, if an advisor can't answer any questions about a client's housing plans after a 45-minute meeting, I'd question how they can make life-changing investment recommendations to that client. How much is their home worth? What do they want to do with their house? Are they moving soon? Where do their kids and grandkids live? Is their goal in retirement to move someplace warmer? These are the questions I started asking, and a whole new world opened its doors to me and my clients.

GETTING THE RIGHT INFORMATION

According to the Ohio State study "Aging in Place,"[2] most participants first learned about a reverse mortgage from a television ad or from friends and family, while only 5% learned from a professional financial advisor! That data reflects what I have experienced in the financial industry, and I know very few advisors who know the intricacies of how reverse mortgages work.

With all the different types of financial advisors you see today, the CFP® designation (Certified Financial Planner) is the gold standard for fiduciary duty and well-roundedness, but the coursework for less known designations like the RICP® (Retirement Income Certified Professional) actually goes into more depth on reverse mortgages. When I first started specializing in reverse mortgages, I gathered a list of local financial advisors and other independent advisors with RICP®s I thought could be good to partner with, and I soon identified part of the reverse mortgage problem: that list wasn't very long.

I found that financial planners and counselors with specific education about reverse mortgage strategy are few and far between.

---

2. Stephanie Moulton, Cäzilia Loibl, et. al "Aging in Place: Analyzing the Use of Reverse Mortgages to Preserve Independent Living," *The Ohio State University*.

My hope is that, with this book, I'm able to help move that needle and get more people the information they need. Moving the needle means educating as many people as possible, both people in the financial space who advise clients and the public, consisting of those currently age-eligible or who will be so they can start planning accordingly now.

Only hearing about reverse mortgages from friends and family or unverified sources on the internet is a big reason why misinformation about reverse mortgages exists.

I recently met with a client who told me a story about somebody she knew in the process of selling their home of over 30 years because ongoing maintenance costs were starting to impact their quality of life. When I told her that through a reverse mortgage, there most certainly would have been another option for this individual, it brought her to tears. She felt terrible that this person wasn't given the full picture of possibilities by people they had talked to. Unfortunately, there are many people out there just like her friend.

But there is a better way. Don't listen to people who simply dole out generic advice. Listen to your gut and your heart when making a big financial decision. Does the advice you're being given meet your actual goals? Were the right questions asked up front for them to know your true intentions? Focus on people who can give specialized advice based on your specific situation. The popular financial gurus with millions of followers may make blanket statements, but I can guarantee you that those statements aren't true for every financial portrait.

Most people, by the time they hit their mid-60s, have spent years and years of their lives waiting in gleeful anticipation for the day the mortgage would be paid off. They've likely made sacrifices to ensure their house was paid off. And when it finally happened, they were very proud, as they should be. Not until after this important milestone do most people feel a little more comfortable spending their liquid savings, because in the back of their minds they plan to leave the house to their children, often by default.

By the time they're eligible, this lifelong focus leaves them feeling like reverse mortgages are counter-intuitive. Even the phrase "reverse mortgage" sounds like an attack on their life's financial work and triggers "debt stress" that overrides logic. Unknowingly, they made a crucial retirement decision when they first got their mortgage, perhaps at age 30, and never revisited how their home financing impacted everything else. Does this sound familiar?

It's critical to break this cycle because after years of inflation and market risk in retirement, the balance sheet gets "off balance." The illiquid real estate asset becomes a much larger percentage of one's overall wealth over time and there isn't enough outside the house to live on, so it gets sold in their 80s or 90s when they are unlikely to want to move from a familiar setting.

Unfortunately, many people don't consider the option of a reverse mortgage.

A lot of advertising for reverse mortgages lists many of the key benefits, but because reverse mortgages already have an image issue, these ads sound gimmicky. Most people still haven't seen the numbers or don't feel they understand the risks, so they bury their heads and hope to never need to learn about it. A social stigma exists around it, as though it's shameful to spend your own money. It's like there's currently a little club of pioneers who have done it and seen those benefits firsthand. At the time of writing, that's about 50,000 people a year.

According to Ohio State's "Aging in Place" study, most who use a reverse mortgage are very happy with their decision after the fact. Actual testimonials are full of folks noting their initial skepticism but that it worked out exactly like they were told it would. They share that they couldn't afford the life they have now without doing a reverse mortgage because they were only using the liquid part of their nest egg.

YOUR FUTURE FINANCIAL HEALTH

Many people have been conditioned not to look at the house as an asset as they transition from accumulation to draw down, but isn't it intuitive that you would? A house is a huge asset on the balance sheet. And even though you might have been told, "Don't view the home as an investment," I don't know many people who decide to buy a house because they think it's going to be a *bad* investment. We look for the best value for our money and typically expect to make money long-term, even though the function or utility of the home is usually the most important factor to consider.

I saw many clients in their seventies who had ongoing debt payments for various reasons and lived on credit cards, yet they had wealth other places they could have been using with less risk.

For many people, a house is their largest asset.

The term "reverse mortgage" itself is a very hotly debated issue, even among professionals who for decades have been helping people secure that very thing. Some reverse mortgage veterans even advise others in the industry not to use those exact words because, in their experience, once you do, many people won't listen because of their preconceived ideas. There have been many attempts to simply rename it something else, but that can come off as deceptive and distasteful.

In my personal experience I think it's the word "mortgage" that makes people nervous, because many people believe that a mortgage equals a principal and or interest payment. The word "reverse" does invoke some caution, as it should, because it's a completely unique loan type and the first time many people have seen one. The youngest person eligible for an FHA-insured HECM is 62 years old, which means, at the time of writing, this person would have been 28 when reverse mortgages first came out. How many 28-year-olds out there know about the newest retirement tools available to them?

When reverse mortgages became more popular before the financial crisis of 2008, there weren't good controls on limits people could borrow and many got in bad situations that gave the loan a bad rap. FHA has since added a financial assessment and more conservative limits.

Reputational risk alone is why some financial professionals feel the need to shy away from the term, and later we'll get into how the history of reverse mortgages created a lot of myths in the larger collective consciousness that we're still working to dispel.

But I made the personal decision to get educated on this topic so that I could educate others because what I saw wasn't fair to the many who had wealth in their homes but were told to look for money elsewhere when they needed it.

DO I NEED A REVERSE MORTGAGE ANALYSIS

The analysis can be looked at in two ways, depending on the purpose you have in mind:

1) Investment View: Equalize a balance sheet for optimal full balance sheet withdraw rate.

This strategy views housing from an investment standpoint. If this is you, you'll view a reverse mortgage through the lens of generating income or maximizing your withdraw efficiency over time in retirement decumulation without having to sell the house to do it. You need to evaluate whether a reverse mortgage is the right solution by looking at your total balance sheet withdraw rate.

2) Shelter Expense View: Minimize lifetime shelter cost from a whole dollar standpoint.

Rather than looking at your housing as an investment, you see it as a cost, because you have to pay for a roof over your head throughout your lifetime anyway. What is your total lifetime housing cost? With this viewpoint, you might use a reverse mortgage to get as much as possible back out from what's been put into the house so far. Using a reverse mortgage with this approach allows you to minimize the amount of money you've sunk into housing, especially if you are looking to spend your money on other things or most of your assets are tied up in housing.

If you view housing as a shelter cost, the utility of a nice roof over your head, then who cares what happens to property values later? In contrast, if you bought it to live in hoping for appreciation, who cares about the rental income you could have earned? If you have other investments, you may not need to maximize the home investment return by paying full price for housing in retirement, which often can mean hundreds of thousands of dollars less! Why pay more?

As I'm only one generation removed from being a farmer, I look at these two purposes for a reverse mortgage like this: "If you are buying a cow for milk, why worry about the price of beef?"

WHY MORE CONSUMERS ARE LOOKING INTO REVERSE MORTGAGES

I'm not the only one with an ever-growing interest in this retirement tool. Demand for reverse mortgages is growing based on demographic shifts and economic realities setting in for retirees. Which means more and more people are going to be talking about them. Retirees are looking for creative ways to increase their income, either because it is limited and they are concerned about the ability for it to last long term, or they want to live better with a strategic financial plan.

According to the Social Security Administration[3], 36 percent of retired Americans rely on Social Security as their only income, while 48 percent of retiree couples rely on it as a primary income. That number jumps to 71 percent for single retirees. But most Social Security checks average less than $1,500 per month. Reverse mortgages offer a solution that lets these individuals live comfortably while still owning their home.

The strategic aspect of reverse mortgages is that they can be designed to help people extend the assets they already have.

3. https://www.ebri.org/docs/default-source/rcs/2021-rcs/rcs_21-fs-2.pdf?sfvrsn=2d83a2f_4

The reality is that life expectancies are continuing to grow, which means after retirement we're looking at financing decades of our lives with what we've accumulated up to that point. People are looking into reverse mortgages because they want to maximize that time and make those decades the best years of their lives while maintaining maximum independence.

WITHDRAW RATE SELF-ANALYSIS

If you're a retiree, you might be familiar with your withdraw rate or portfolio burn rate: the amount you can safely withdraw from your savings and investments to live on based on your life expectancy. An interesting concept to consider is what your total net worth/full balance sheet withdraw rate would be, rather than only considering withdrawals from your liquid savings. A fun exercise, explained below, is to calculate your short balance sheet withdraw rate, which can be done on the back of an envelope or napkin, as a measure for your personal performance converting from accumulator to decumulator. The lower the withdraw rate, the more likely someone may feel they are living below their means relative to those around them with similar total net worth. In essence, if someone invested more of their lifetime earnings into a bigger house, they may live poorer than their neighbors later. They're using only a fraction of their total accumulation to live on. It's about cashflow. The reverse mortgage is the balance sheet equalizer because it frees up cash flow.

1. Complete a simple reverse mortgage assessment to ensure you understand your net worth and withdraw rate. You can begin by using the assessment tools below.
2. Write down a couple key words of what triggered the idea of reverse mortgage for you. This is important to write down early without thinking much, and you'll return to it later.

We want to be sure that we don't get too far away from what that initial thought was when we start digging in.

3. Ask yourself, "What stress is alleviated by the idea of a reverse mortgage and what new stresses does it create?" Writing these down allows you to focus your questions and concerns for the counselor and loan officer to address.
4. Create your own short balance sheet and your own short income statement for a simple retirement assessment. Use last year's withdrawals because these will be most indicative of your near future spending needs, excluding one-time expenses.

By short balance sheet and short income statement, I mean listing major assets and income items that could be done on the back of an envelope, not needing to list every minor detail to get an estimate for yourself. When assessing your withdraw rate, it's important to measure your internal income—income that is generated with your own assets, unlike external income, which is generated from external sources such as a job, social security, or any pensions. Your internal income indicates the lifestyle and net worth you've already worked for and is separate from your external sources.

For example, say you have two people who both have a net worth of $1.3 million. The first has liquid assets of $1 million while $300,000 is tied up in their house with approximately $50,000 of internal income generated at a 5% portfolio withdraw rate. The second has a house worth $1 million and only $300,000 of liquid assets with approximately $15,000 of internal income generated at a 5% portfolio withdraw rate. The first person is able to live a much better lifestyle than the second person because the withdraw rate on their total accumulated assets or on their total balance sheet is lower.

In other words, measure your withdraw rate to determine how well have you converted your assets into income.

(This is not financial advice. I recommend you consult with a professional advisor to evaluate your distinct situation.)

Short Balance Sheet

Assets

Total illiquid assets (primary residence, real estate/land) + total liquid assets (bank accounts, CDs, savings, investment account, 401K, 403Bs) =____________________________

Total assets = ______________________________

Liabilities

Total mortgage balances + credit card balances + auto loans + other liabilities = ________________________

Total liabilities = ___________________

Total assets – total liabilities = **Net Worth**

Short Income Statement

Internal Income (portfolio capital gains, rental income, investment dividends, interest, RMDs/portfolio withdraws) = _______________

Short Balance Sheet Withdraw Rate Example

Total Net Worth (e.g., $1,500,000 total assets ($800,000 house + $400,000 rental home + $300,000 investment assets/savings) - $100,000 Debt ($20,000 auto + $80,000 mortgage) = **$1,400,000 Net Worth**

Total Internal Income (e.g., $2000 Rental Income + $2000 portfolio/month) = $4,000/month or **$48,000/year**

Total Internal Income/Total Net Worth = $48,000/$1,400,000

Short Balance Sheet Withdraw Rate = 3.4%

Traditional Portfolio Withdraw Rate: $24,000 *($2,000/month)/**$300,000** portfolio =* ***8%***

(With these numbers, based on the traditional portfolio withdraw rate, you will likely be told you are living too large! Talk to your advisor about what you can do to improve your total balance sheet withdraw rate.)

With these figures on paper, it becomes very clear what your biggest assets are and where resources exist that you can draw on. If there's a deficit or shortfall in one place, where can you pull from? What's the annual cost of each of your assets and is there any safe leverage available to equalize things?

MAXIMIZING YOUR RETIREMENT YEARS WITH A REVERSE MORTGAGE

A lot of people think that retirement is some magical transition, as if you wake up the day after you retire, and everything is different. That's just not the case. You wake up to the same feelings, personality, and problems you had before, just usually with less money coming in. You may have different ways you think you'll spend your time, but this new life trajectory isn't going to happen without turning the wheel a little to change the ship's course. You'll have to actively pursue new activities and it can take a few years to get the hang of it.

You must set up ways to hold yourself accountable to achieve these new life goals. If you want to comfortably visit your son and his kids, what can you do to make that happen? If you want to have big family vacations, how can you set yourself up for success? I've seen parents use a reverse mortgage to buy a condo for their daughter who was a single mom and schoolteacher. This gave them tremendous peace of mind and allowed them to enjoy the time they had *now* with their child and grandkids rather than leaving her their house at some date way down the road. She has a beautiful home with her children and will also get any appreciation that occurs on the condo.

I've also seen retired couples maximize retirement by using a reverse mortgage to purchase a vacation property, either for themselves or for the whole family to enjoy during holidays and school breaks. In fact, one older couple I know in Phoenix saw this as their main goal in retirement. They always thought their retirement would include big family get-togethers with all their kids and grandkids in one place. But it wasn't happening because the numbers they ran on paper never seemed to add up to what they were really spending. They leveraged the equity in their current home to buy a ranch in Flagstaff. Now the whole extended family has a lovely vacation home they can enjoy together, all paid for by a portion of the equity in their primary home, and they can keep the appreciation on both properties and pay off the balance on the reverse mortgage when they permanently leave their own primary residence.

I've seen similar approaches play out with charitable giving, too. Folks who planned to give everything to charity were able to see the seeds of their contributions flourish in life rather than waiting until after they passed. Whether buying a home for a specific nonprofit or donating cash, this is a great option for those who feel strongly about giving. Although it gets into some advanced planning techniques, you could consider charitable contribution bunching strategies, where charitable contributions are high enough in one single year to allow for impressive tax benefits. Note: you'll want to consult a financial planner or experienced tax professional about these benefits.

In the next chapter, we'll go more in-depth on the requirements and the step-by-step process of getting the reverse mortgage that could be the very tool you need to maximize your own retirement.

REVERSE MORTGAGES IN REAL LIFE

An adult child becoming the primary caregiver for a parent who is aging in place is a common scenario in our country. According to the Center for Retirement Research at Boston College, about 17 percent of adult children care for their parents at some point in their lives, and the likelihood of doing so rises with age.

This was the case for mother and daughter Alma and Shelley. Alma owned her home in New Buffalo, Michigan, and as it became clear that she required more dedicated care, Shelley moved back in with her.

Shelley, who was in her early 60s, had to quit her job to take on this full-time caregiver role. While she didn't have a housing payment while living with her mom, she still had living expenses. She was living off her widowed mother's income and assets. But it wasn't enough.

Originally, her thought was that once her mom died, she would get the house. But with a reverse mortgage, she was able to use that money sooner, knowing that in exchange, she'd get less money later.

This is the perfect option for individuals like this mother-daughter duo who were house-rich and cash-poor. In this situation, Shelley still wanted to inherit her mother's house. Because she was over 62, Shelley and Alma simply entered the loan together in a trust where both were primary beneficiaries. When Alma dies, Shelley can continue to live in the house for the rest of her life. In the meantime, Alma can use the funds from the reverse mortgage to essentially pay her daughter to work as her caregiver. She thinks of it as "fronting" Shelley's inheritance, making it doable for both to live a comfortable life *now*.

Most people who are put in the situation of becoming the primary caregiver for an aging parent aren't necessarily independently wealthy. They may not have money lying around to live on when they drop everything to go care for Mom or Dad. And if their parent lives longer than they expected when they first took on the role of caregiver, funds may become depleted right when healthcare costs are skyrocketing. Reverse mortgages offer a way forward for families like Shelley and Alma.

— 4 —

GETTING A REVERSE MORTGAGE

United States Government-insured reverse mortgages make up over 90% of the reverse mortgage market. The Federal Housing Administration's reverse mortgage program is known as the Home Equity Conversion Mortgage (HECM).

A HECM allows you to convert a portion of the existing equity you have in your home, whether you have an existing mortgage or not.

FHA dictates exactly how much you can get out based on age, interest rates, and appraised value. It's a cash loan, simply using the house as collateral. You then choose how you want to withdraw these funds: as a lump sum, a fixed income stream for a period of time or life, incrementally, or simply as needed in a standby line of credit. In some cases, you can change your election as your needs change throughout retirement. HECMs can also be used to purchase a primary residence through a product called the HECM-for-Purchase (more on that later).

The other 10% of reverse mortgages are called proprietary reverse mortgages, which follow many of the same standards and processes as the HECM but may not have all the same guarantees a HECM provides so it's imperative that you know the differences. There are some cases where a proprietary reverse mortgage, sometimes known as a Jumbo Reverse, is a better fit.

Jumbo Reverse Benefits:

1. Issued as low as age 55 in some states
2. Allow higher value properties to be leveraged
3. Can offer a higher percentage of equity made available
4. No upfront or ongoing Mortgage Insurance Premium (MIP)
5. Non-recourse loan
6. Can consolidate consumer debt with the mortgage itself to qualify

Jumbo Reverse Drawbacks:

1. Higher interest rates to offset the risk of not having FHA safety net
2. Minimum property values that may be as high as $400,000
3. Sometimes require carrying a minimum loan balance
4. May not have protections for non-borrowing spouses
5. Lines of credit growth may be capped
6. Some lenders require circumstances to not fit a HECM before applying for a proprietary

HECM (HOME EQUITY CONVERSION MORTGAGE) ELIGIBILITY

To be eligible for a Home Equity Conversion Mortgage, you must meet the following criteria:

- One borrower must be 62 years of age or older.

- You must occupy the property as your primary place of residence.
- You should not be delinquent on any federal debt or housing charges (This may not disqualify you, but tell your lender about the delinquency up front.)
- You must participate in a mandatory credit counseling session with an HUD-approved counselor to ensure disclosures were made and the borrower understands how it works.
- There needs to be enough equity in the home to cover any existing liens (mortgage, solar, HELOC, mechanics lien) or a free and clear title. (If there isn't enough equity in the home, borrowers have the ability to come in with other assets.)

WHAT'S THE PROCESS FOR A HECM?

Once you've determined a reverse mortgage could be beneficial and have confirmed your eligibility, what's next? The first step in the process is to talk to a reverse mortgage advisor or loan officer to find out what's available and how much equity you may have access to. Let's walk through the entire process, from first consultation to closing, to give you an overview of how it usually plays out.

Step 1: Consultation With a Reverse Mortgage Advisor/Loan Officer

A qualified loan officer will get a better understanding of what your situation is and walk you through a financial review that involves details about your goals and your property, including how long you've owned the home and what your intent for the home is in the future. It's also important for the loan officer to understand who all the interested parties are, whether there is an eligible spouse, children to consider, or Powers of Attorney, as well as if the property is in a trust. Also disclose any recent adverse credit concerns and outstanding debt so the loan officer knows how best to structure things from the beginning.

Note: Any loan officer can do forward and reverse loans. However, many forward-only loan officers transition to try to do reverse mortgages when rates go up and their regular business dries up, so make sure the person you are working with knows the reverse mortgage process well and does them regularly.

From this initial conversation, a proposal can be generated. This is a non-binding proposal because no formal applications have been signed and submitted yet. It allows the borrowers to see the following:

1. Their loan product options given the current interest rates and property value estimate
2. Estimated closing costs and total annual loan cost (TALC)
3. At least three different HECM rate options and applicable proprietary product options
4. Applicable required consumer disclosures
5. A unique counseling code

At this point, the borrower still doesn't have to make up their mind on what they're going to do but can move forward if they are interested.

Rates and borrowing limits typically are floating until closing so make sure you are aware of which way rates may be headed as you wait. The rates don't lock as early as conventional mortgages. The secondary market isn't big enough yet for investors to buy them in bulk at different rates. Sometimes the loan may take months to close if there are extraordinary circumstances throughout the process.

Step 2: HUD-Approved Counseling

Before obtaining a HECM, you are required to receive counseling from an independent, HUD-approved counselor. This is a great safeguard built right into the process that ensures you receive all the facts you need to make an informed decision before moving forward with the process. HUD maintains a list[4] on their website of all certified counselors in the country for easy access and selection.

Typically, a HUD-approved counselor is not a formal financial professional but may have a social work background or have worked for a nonprofit credit counseling agency. They undergo a certification process through the U.S. Department of Housing and Urban Development to effectively counsel potential borrowers on the ins and outs of reverse mortgages. They may also provide other types of financial or housing counseling. The charge for the counseling can vary but it tends to be between $125-$200, which the borrowers must pay out of pocket. However, sometimes it can run upwards of $300, depending on the area.

Thanks to the comprehensive list of counselors, consumers can shop around. But some proprietary lenders require certain agencies, so double-check with your loan officer that you have the right list. As you check out their listings, you'll see that some agencies are virtual, and some are local and in-person. Many people opt to do their sessions over the phone. Usually, the counseling takes about 45 minutes to an hour and all parties subject to the loan must be present for the duration of the session, although the loan officer will not be present to maintain impartiality. If there are multiple trustees, you could have a lot of people in a meeting or on a call. Anyone subject or party to the title or the loan must be listed on that counseling

4. https://www.hudexchange.info/programs/housing-counseling/hecm/origination/#hud-intermediaries-providing-hecm-counseling-nationwide

form or it can delay the process. Additionally, any interested party like a beneficiary or child can also be on the call.

The counselor wants to make sure you have all the facts when it comes to your reverse mortgage. Generally, they'll go over the costs of setting up the loan, the ongoing costs and requirements to maintaining the loan, what happens when it becomes due and payable, and answers to any questions you have. They'll reiterate the structure of a negatively amortizing loan and help you understand the process for getting out of a loan like this one. Your loan officer should not steer you to one agency over another.

Once a counseling session has been completed, your HUD-approved counselor will issue you a certificate that is good for 180 days. To move forward with the lending process, you will need a completed Certificate of HECM Counseling that is signed and dated by the counselor and current (within that 180-day period). You can use your completed counseling certificate at multiple lenders if you aren't fully committed. Just because you start the process with one loan officer doesn't mean you can't switch after counseling.

However, if you are already working with a reverse mortgage advisor or loan officer to generate a proposal, most counseling agencies simply send the completed and signed certificate right to them using the unique counseling code that was generated in the proposal. As the borrower, you don't have to deal with it. It goes right to the lender. From there, your lender can gather the documents needed to submit a formal application.

Step 3: Application

Once the counseling is done and application submitted, the lender can order services (title search, attorney reviews, appraisal). In most states, nothing can be ordered other than a credit check until after counseling happens and a lender has that certificate in hand.

Your loan officer pulls your credit prior to application or at application. Credit underwriting for a reverse mortgage is a little bit different than your standard forward mortgage in the sense that they're not underwriting your ability as the borrower to repay the loan with your income and assets. Lenders are mainly looking only at a person's ability to pay their ongoing property charge obligations rather than making payments on the loan balance itself. This is one of the first areas that feels very different from any type of loan you've likely seen before.

Your loan officer will be looking at your ability to pay home insurance, property taxes, any HOA fees, and any debts you might have. They'll also look at property payment histories to make sure there haven't been any missed payments in the last 12 months. (If you know about missed payments, bring this up with your loan officer beforehand to discuss possible remedies.)

Additionally, as with any government loan, there's a federal database that is surveyed and pulled to make sure there's no outstanding federal debt that would have to be paid off ahead of time, such as a federal lien. Remember, eligibility can be delayed for certain types of federal liens or active bankruptcy proceedings, but generally workarounds are much more forgiving than a conventional mortgage so don't let that dissuade you from looking into it.

Step 4: Financial Assessment

To help safeguard the long-term success of your HECM over time, the Reverse Mortgage Stabilization Act of 2013 mandated a financial assessment that measures capacity and willingness to meet the ongoing obligations of the loan. Completing the residual income analysis is typically done by your lender behind the scenes, who will let you know if there are any issues and possible resolutions to those issues. In some cases, other resources may need to be considered or other debt paid down. A similar analysis is completed for proprietary reverse mortgages, but because they aren't FHA insured, they don't have to follow every FHA step.

Based on your monthly debt obligations and everything known about the property (e.g., taxes, insurance, utilities estimate, HOA, assessments, etc.), the government (or lender) determines what amount of money you need to have left over each month. This amount varies by region but is typically around $550 for single adults and around $950 for a family of two. Most people meet this threshold based on their social security statements alone. The purpose of this analysis is to determine the capacity of the borrowers to meet their documented financial obligations with their documented income. Combined with the credit history review, this is a required step to determine whether and under what conditions the HECM applicant meets FHA eligibility criteria.

Life Expectancy Set Aside (LESA)

Payment disruptions to property charges, existing debt, or financial assessment failure because of monthly obligations doesn't outright disqualify someone from using a reverse mortgage. If you fail the financial assessment, your lender will determine if a Life Expectancy Set Aside (LESA) is required as a condition of obtaining your HECM. This is a pool of otherwise available home equity set aside in escrow that your servicer will use to pay your property taxes and insurance for the duration of life expectancy. The amount is set by an FHA life expectancy formula[5], which you can estimate with the following formula:

Hypothetical Example:

Age 95 – Current Age = Longevity (for calculation purposes),

(Longevity in years) x (Annual Property Tax and Homeowners Insurance) = Approximate **LESA**

It's not a punishment or a bad thing to have a LESA—it simply means that because you've had some issues paying something in the past, the lender and FHA can't afford to take that risk going forward, so they'll use the set aside funds to take care of the property tax, insurance, and any HOA fees.

Regardless of past credit issues, some borrowers even opt into a LESA because they're worried about missing payments or overspending, which can happen as they grow older. It's a helpful option that your loan officer can discuss with you in more depth.

5. You can find the LESA formula at https://.hud.gov/sites/documents/13-28MLATCH.PDF

Unlike traditional forward mortgages, the lender is not evaluating your ability to repay the principal and interest for 30 years, because you don't have to make payments while using the loan. In some cases, you wouldn't even have to show more than a single bank statement to verify deposits, if you meet the government-set residual income standards.

If that residual income isn't met, that's when your lender will look into other assets. They may look at a savings account or IRA and earmark that for dissipation, meaning those assets could be considered "income" based on an FHA formula.

For example, if you have $100,000 in an IRA, they might earmark $388/month from that account to count toward your income, which may help meet your residual income requirement. This is calculated based on 70% of the value of the asset with an FHA life expectancy table, based on the age of the youngest borrower.

Now that your loan officer has looked at your credit reports, ongoing property obligations (i.e., property tax statements), and monthly residual income; they will submit an application packet. From there, your mortgage will enter the processing/underwriting stage, which can take 15-60 days on average. This is when the lender can order the property appraisal, which will help to determine your maximum claim amount or the amount you can borrow.

Step 5: Property Appraisal

The appraisal can be the longest period in the whole process simply because there tend to be fewer appraisers available to do the work than are needed. A borrower could wait a few weeks before they're able to get an appraisal. Stay patient; it's not personal and doesn't mean anything is wrong. It is not uncommon for your lender to gather your credit card information with your application. They cannot accept cash from borrowers and the appraisal cannot be ordered until the payment method is provided. This process is similar whether you're applying for a HECM or a proprietary loan. In some cases it may be possible to finance the appraisal cost into the final loan costs so discuss your options with your lender.

Now you've paid for counseling, had your credit pulled, and applied for the loan, but you must wait for these final pieces to fall into place. It's also possible that even once your initial appraisal is completed, the FHA may require a second appraisal, called a Collateral Risk Assessment (CRA). This can add another week or two to the process. Unfortunately, this is something that neither the lender nor borrower has any control over. The cost of the second appraisal technically falls to the client but sometimes a lender can provide an offsetting credit depending on the loan structure. It's estimated that 15-20% of homes require a CRA and it is based on random selection. All lenders require a second appraisal for any property over $2M.

An appraiser's job is to determine the market value of your home at the time of appraisal.

With most residential homes, there are a few different methods an appraiser can use to generate an appraisal depending on the use of the property and location. Typically for refinance loans, they are looking at recent sales comparisons in the immediate area or "comps" to determine a range. From there, they'll start adding or subtracting value based on any updates completed or updates that are needed. This can be difficult to determine in areas where many houses haven't sold for a while, or where the area is a patchwork of different types of custom homes. You can see what all the houses around you sold for on the surface, but maybe they were renovated, so it's never a direct comparison.

While it isn't always the case, an appraisal for the same home on a purchase contract may come in higher than a house that is not for sale. This is because an offer in the hand is better than an offer in the bush, as it were. When selling your home, you may value your house at $500,000, but if you have a signed sales contract showing someone's willingness to pay $550,000, the appraisal will likely come in at $550,000 if it is justified. During the reverse mortgage appraisal process, there's no purchase contract in place to show what someone is truly willing to pay, so the value can come in different than what you may expect. Nonetheless, your appraiser will do a thorough job evaluating your home's square footage, lot size, and location to determine appropriate value.

Step 6: Processing and Clear to Close Approval

After the appraisal evaluation process and all other legal reviews, documents, and verifications have been processed, your reverse mortgage leaves the processing stage and moves into the final underwriting approval process. This is when the lender formally approves you and your property for the loan! All your documents are reviewed, finalized, and prepared for closing by a processor in coordination with the title company throughout this process. The lender makes sure that the loan and all documents associated with it will be accepted by a subsequent investor if being sold. All these people behind the scenes are what most of your closing costs pay for. An excellent title company and excellent processing team can make a tremendous difference in a borrower's overall experience.

The job to follow up with the borrower is typically split between the loan officer and the processing team, just like a forward mortgage. They will reach out to you if they need any additional documentation. If the processor can't get a hold of the borrower, then they may return to the loan officer to reach out on their behalf.

A reverse mortgage closes in the same amount of time as a traditional mortgage, typically 30-60 days. Your loan officer should be able to foresee potential delay areas and have a good contingency plan in place.

Step 7: Closing and Payout Election

The loan is signed with a notary, at your home, office, or prescheduled location just like with a conventional forward mortgage. Your loan officer is not required but may elect to be present at signing to answer any last-minute questions or interpret any documents. The notary will have all the documents in-hand that require your signature, but they are not a licensed loan officer, so they are not able to interpret any of the documents, only state what they are. There will be documents your loan officer needs to sign, but that can be done separately. After signing your closing documents, you have a grace period of three days, per federal law, wherein you can still cancel the loan without penalty if you so choose. This is known as a rescission period.

Your funds are disbursed based on your previously decided payout election. On adjustable-rate loans, you may be able to change your election after closing, although on fixed-rate loans, there are no draws/changes after closing and a refinance may be needed to restructure the loan. You may see them described in various formats, but the detailed payout plan options are as follows:

- **Lump Sum** – You receive maximum available funds. (Limits may apply.)
- **Partial Lump Sum** – You elect to receive only a portion of your maximum available funds amount. (Limits may apply.)
- **Term** – You receive fixed monthly payments for a fixed period of months.
- **Modified Term** – You receive fixed monthly payments for a fixed period of months and a line of credit.
- **Tenure** – You receive all funds in fixed monthly payments for the entire life of the loan.
- **Modified Tenure** – You receive a lower fixed monthly payment, and the difference goes into a line of credit for the entire life of the loan.
- **Line of Credit** – Your funds are available upon request from the servicer. (Plan to not have access for up to 60 days after closing while the loan is onboarded and consider having any funds you may need in the short-term to be withdrawn at closing if imperative.)

Payout Election

When your loan officer draws up your proposal, they'll outline all the different payout options so you can decide up front. Think of the payout election as instructions to the lender. The lender needs to know where to send the money. If you're using your HECM or reverse mortgage to pay off an existing mortgage, you would elect for the money to go there. Whereas if you're using it as a line of credit, the lender doesn't have to send it anywhere. You could even elect a term payment, where the funds are paid out over a predetermined period of time, which can be a great financial planning tool to build income bridges for specific purposes. Whatever the case may be, those numbers will be outlined in your initial proposal and fine-tuned about a week out from closing when make your election.

Once your closing is complete, you will never again have to make a mortgage payment on your home as long as you occupy it as your primary residence and remain current on property taxes, insurance, home maintenance costs, and HOA fees.

Disbursement Limits

There is an initial disbursement limit on all Home Equity Conversion Mortgages, which has been set as a safeguard for equity protection and serves almost as a built-in cooling off period. The limit was enacted in 2013 as a response to research obtained when evaluating the risk of the overall HECM program. The government analyzed foreclosure data from the financial crisis only a few years earlier and noticed the highest foreclosure rates (mostly technical default due to delinquent property taxes) were highly correlated with the amount drawn at closing. The higher initial draws tended to have higher foreclosure risk, almost a "take the money and run" mindset.

This limitation applies for the first 12 months of the loan, ending after the one-year anniversary of closing. The maximum disbursement within that time frame is 60% of the available Principal Loan Limit (some exceptions based on payoffs may apply).

Most proprietary reverse mortgages have their own nuances to how they handle Principal Loan Limits, which should be considered by your loan officer when selecting suitable products at the proposal phase.

HECM FOR PURCHASE

The HECM for Purchase (H4P) program was rolled out by the FHA in 2009. Prior to that, retirees would have to pay cash to buy a house, then do a reverse mortgage afterward to get some of the capital back out in two separate transactions. That meant borrowers incurred extra costs of accessing that much cash or even depleting emergency funds for several months. The H4P allows you to purchase a home, with only a fraction down, in a single transaction! It's a program I personally plan to take advantage of as soon as I can because I don't want to sink that much cash into a house, yet I also don't want a mortgage payment.

This program is a boon for people who were lucky enough to know someone to teach them about it. Most people would love to transfer the risk to a bank and use their cash at a capped or fixed rate, but they associate mortgages with debt and debt with payment or risk. The H4P allows more financial security in the sense that it preserves liquid assets to be used as a buffer to the stock market or a rescue boat to the whole balance sheet during stagflation when everything else is down.

H4P Example:

A 70-year-old borrower could find a nice house for $500,000 they want to buy in Sun City. They can pay cash if they want and simply have monthly housing payments of around $400.

Alternatively, they could buy the exact same house and put approximately $300,000 down and still only have a monthly housing payment of $400 a month. But they pocket the additional $200,000. Maybe they buy some nice furniture for entertaining if that's of value to them. Maybe they take an extra annual golf trip or a world cruise.

As another option, they could find a house selling for $800,000 that's more in line with what they want, maybe closer to family, important activities, and medical buildings. They never thought they'd be able to live in that neighborhood because they never spent that much on a house while they were working. But with H4P they only have to put down about $425,000. That'd be a big housing upgrade and they'd still pocket an additional $75,000!

It's a real disservice not letting people know reverse mortgages are available to leverage their own wealth and preserve liquid assets.

If you want to use a HECM to purchase a house, consult with your loan officer as soon as possible in the process and they'll be able to guide you as to what the underwriters and real estate agent are going to require. Those requirements may vary by state and are ever-changing. Most of the requirements are the same, but one big difference that likely won't change is the inability for sellers to offer concessions beyond what is customary for the area. That is sensible because FHA doesn't want the "collateral" price inflated artificially by other things.

HECM for purchase combines a reverse mortgage loan with the equity from the sale of your previous home (or other assets and savings) to buy your next primary residence in one transaction. Just like you do on an existing house, with a reverse mortgage of any kind you need to make sure the collateral is protected and maintain it. You must pay your annual property taxes and homeowners' insurance as well as maintain the property as a primary residence; but you only make one initial payment toward your purchase—no monthly mortgage payments needed.

Do you want to leverage your house to pay for the house, or do you want to leverage your income or other assets to pay for the house? That's your choice.

Closing costs are similar between conventional forward mortgages and reverse mortgages, but you pay FHA insurance with a reverse mortgage that you may not with a conventional loan that isn't government-backed. You're borrowing money both ways; there's an interest rate both ways—the structure is simply different. With a reverse mortgage, you get the benefit of using low-risk leverage with a bank against a stable asset and it can protect you from having to tap into your portfolio while it's down, beyond any mandatory withdraws.

HOW MUCH CAN YOU BORROW?

Maximum Claim Amount

The value of your home, generated by the appraiser, will generally be used as the maximum claim amount (MCA). It's what FHA will reimburse the lender if somehow the value didn't hold up later. The amount you can borrow is then based off the MCA, or appraised value.

The 2022 reverse mortgage limit set by the FHA is currently $970,800. If your house is valued at a number higher than that limit, your maximum claim amount would top out at $970,800.

FHA uses a life expectancy table that runs through ages 99 and older to determine the percentage someone can borrow. The older you are, the higher the percentage of equity you can access because mathematically there aren't as many likely years for interest to accrue until repayment. The going interest rate, or current cost of money at the time, will also dictate how much someone can borrow at each age level. Although the current rate index used for interest accrual is the one-year CMT, FHA looks out at the future to calculate the likely cost of capital, or interest rate, over the likely life of the loan. Most loans last about 10 years, reverses included, so the FHA table uses an expected rate off of the 10-year CMT, which is normally higher than the one-year rate in a normal interest rate environment.

> Example: The current one-year CMT is at 2% and current 10-year treasury is 4%. FHA will assume the rate is 4% now to determine that initial "Principal Limit." As the 10-year drops, let's say to 3%, the future cost of capital is projected to be lower, and the interest rate is likely lower, meaning less accrued interest, so a higher percentage becomes available for people locking in loan terms at that time.

Planning note: Many borrowers in appreciating areas will refinance to capture a higher available loan amount, because every year they get older a higher amount becomes available, and as the property goes up in value, that can be locked in as well. Rising interest rates make it much more important to forecast medium-term interest costs to give yourself a nice buffer to weather a long-term economic downturn and minimize what's called sequence of returns risk.

The older the borrower, the lower the interest rates, and the greater the home value, the greater the available funds will be.

Principal Loan Limit

A Principal Loan Limit (PLL) is the amount a borrower is eligible to access, and it is a percentage of your MCA. It is made available as funds to you and is established at closing.

The PLL is determined by taking these things into consideration:

- Age of youngest borrower or non-borrowing spouse
- Maximum claim amount (appraised value)
- Expected interest rate (10-year treasury rate)

Note that the expected interest rate and principal loan limit is locked on the day the borrower signs their application, but the actual starting accrual rate will float until closing. That's because investors don't want to commit money to buy loans until they know the cost. Most lenders try to honor rates at application, but only if the market dictates. If interest rates are volatile, discuss with your loan officer your ability to access more if rates were to drop further by closing.

Fixed vs. Adjustable Rate Mortgages

There are two primary types of reverse mortgage structures: Fixed (closed-ended loan) and Adjustable Rate (open-ended loan). As you've learned, there are many end goals to this type of loan and considering yours will help you identify which rate structure is best for you. The different reverse mortgage structures and rates can serve different purposes and outcomes.

Fixed Rate

A fixed rate loan transfers the future interest rate risk to the lender. If rates go up later, they lose the ability to loan those funds at the higher rate. A reverse mortgage with a fixed rate allows you one-time access to all your loan proceeds at closing. Once any existing mortgages or liens on the property are taken care of, plus an allowance in some cases, you are paid out in a single lump sum.

FHA determines the amount you can receive at closing, and your reverse mortgage advisor/loan officer can walk you through the exact numbers for your situation.

If you choose a fixed rate reverse mortgage, it's important to determine whether the borrowed amount is adequate to meet your end goal. With a fixed rate, you'll accrue interest on the entire loan balance, which starts at the closing of the loan.

I speak more often about fixed rate loans with people who are using them to pay off old forward mortgages. They still want the reassurance of knowing exactly what the amortization table looks like and what interest will accrue for planning purposes.

Adjustable Rate

A reverse mortgage with an adjustable rate offers much more flexibility. With an adjustable rate, it's open-ended, so future draws are allowed. Any funds not available at closing or within the first 12 months are accessible to you after 12 months.

Adjustable rate reverse mortgages are still very common even though they float, because the current rate is typically lower than a fixed rate would be and it's capped even when rates go up. Adjustable rate reverse mortgages come with a built in line of credit for unused funds and offer a lot of flexibility to draw or delay.

An adjustable rate affords you the option to receive your home equity in those different forms like monthly, tenure, and term payments, or you can choose to take only a portion of available funds and leave the difference in a line of credit. The interest rate is usually capped at either 5 or 10% from where it starts depending on the product you choose. The one-year CMT index is the only adjustable part of the rate, so it provides a level of reassurance knowing it's tied to the U.S. economy and housing market.

Choosing Your Rate

One of the most important decisions to make with the reverse mortgage is what type of rate you choose. Because each rate type has a different loan structure, sometimes the situation or use dictates what you will go with.

A fixed rate gives you all the funds available in one fell swoop, while the adjustable rate gives you a line of credit and allows you to choose how much money you want to receive at any given time. The rest of the funds can stay available in case a need arises.

With either rate option, prepayment isn't penalized. You can always pay back funds you didn't end up needing or make elective payments, but the rate type will determine what happens to future payments. With the adjustable rate, when you make a payment, it will increase your future line of credit dollar for dollar, while the fixed rate option will still pay down the balance, but the funds will not be available again without refinancing or selling the house.

Fixed Rate Hypothetical Example

Let's say your home is valued at $600,000 and you are approved for a reverse mortgage that gives you access to 50% of that amount, a principal limit of $300,000. However, if you select a fixed rate, because there are first year withdraw limits, you only have access to 60% of that or $180,000. While you're locking in an interest rate for the life of the loan and know the interest accrual with certainty, you can only get cash out once. There are exceptions with higher initial fixed rate draws, but they're only available to pay off any existing liens.

You have an existing mortgage balance of $150,000 on that $600,000 house and your goal is to eliminate your mortgage with a plan of staying in your home. You are eligible to borrow $180,000. So, you have a choice: you could just borrow the $150,000 you need, or you could borrow the full amount and eliminate the remaining mortgage payment *and* have $30,000 in cash sent to your bank at closing. All at the same interest rate, locked in indefinitely.

If you chose to only take out the $150,000 and decided later that you needed more, you would have to do another reverse mortgage to get more money out.

Adjustable Rate Hypothetical Example

However, with an adjustable rate structure, you'd have a comparable principal loan limit of $300,000, which would all become available after the first year. Here you have two options: a 5% cap and a 10% cap. The higher the cap, the higher the interest rate can go. Using the same numbers as above, you could take out the $150,000 to pay off your existing mortgage and say, "We don't know if we need that extra $30,000 yet. But we might." So, you simply keep that line of credit available.

The $150,000 balance grows at whatever the adjustable rate is—let's say 3%—but the line of credit *also* grows at that adjustable rate.

Now, say there's a scenario where someone doesn't even need any money upfront. They may say, "Give me the highest rate available," because they want that line of credit to grow as fast as possible for some future use.

The line of credit remains open and active. It can't get cancelled. It can't get frozen. It can't be reduced. It is guaranteed to grow as long as you live in the house.

Rate	Home Value	Principal Limit	60% Year 1 Withdraw Limit	Existing Lien	Cash available at closing	Access lost after closing	Line of Credit Year 1	Line of Credit After Year 1
FIXED	$600,000	$300,000	$180,000	$150,000	$30,000	$150,000	$0	$0
ADJUSTABLE	$600,000	$300,000	$180,000	$150,000	$30,000	$0	$30,000	$150,000

*The entire Principal Limit balance can be used in year 1 if paying off existing liens

REVERSE MORTGAGES IN REAL LIFE

Bradley and Hattie's home is completely paid off and they have legacy goals. They want to be able to leave something to their kids and grandkids.

Their home in Albuquerque, New Mexico, was valued at $800,000. They decided to use a reverse mortgage to get $300,000 of equity out of that home and use the money to buy a condo in Destin, Florida, with cash. Their primary residence is still their beautiful home in Albuquerque. They simply leveraged the equity in that home to buy another one.

The cost was a 5.5% interest rate on $300,000. Now, they're getting appreciation on two different homes in two different states.

They still have legacy goals. And selling both these homes down the line figures into their overall strategy. But they also have current goals, and those have been realized thanks to this second home near the beach.

Think of the possibilities here. In a similar situation, if Bradley and Hattie had a handful of grandchildren who all planned on attending Arizona State University, they could enact the same strategy to purchase a condo in Tempe that they'd keep for eight years as all the kids got their degrees. Their grandchildren could live in the condo rent-free while attending college, and once they'd all graduated, they could sell the condo to pay off the HECM or do something else with the proceeds. There are many ways a reverse mortgage can be a creative solution to your retirement goals.

— 5 —

THE HISTORY OF REVERSE MORTGAGES

The *real* beginning of the real story of reverse mortgages dates back to the late 1920s and the lead up to the Great Depression. Housing financing hadn't fully developed and there was very little regulation. Most loans were up to five years in length, required down payments of at least 50%, and had a balloon payment at the end of the term. Banks and lenders were happy to take the down payment and the house at the end of the term if anything went wrong for the borrower. Even how payments were due was different, often annually. Imagine your 30-year conventional mortgage, but instead of having a $2,000 monthly mortgage payment on a $400,000 house, you had to pay a lump sum of $24,000 every December or you'd lose the house? The money set aside to go toward that payment might start burning a hole in your pocket a few months out. It was a risky proposition.

Consider having to come up with $250,000 cash in five years or you'd lose the house, or paying $50,000 over five years with $200,000 due at the end of the term. You can see why Americans have it in their blood to be skeptical of mixing banks and houses. This was also the time before mainstream secondary loan markets on Wall Street, government agencies like FHA or HUD, or government intervention insuring and funding housing through enterprises like Fannie Mae and Ginnie Mae.

As the economy began to turn, many people lost homes to lenders and financing was hard to find anywhere.

One of the direct responses to this crisis was the creation of the Federal Housing Administration in 1934 to create and manage a government-backed insurance fund and standardize regulatory framework for residential lending. This meant even longer terms available from 5 years for up to 15 years. The government wasn't doing this as pure charity, either. They knew a longer loan term would soften the blow of eventually rising interest rates, paying for the government expansion. Fifteen years gave them a lot of wiggle room.

Traction was slow because there was a justifiable distrust of "housing finance schemes" and it sounded almost too good to be true. To only have to put 20% down, be able to live in the house, make monthly payments over 15 years, and the lender would be okay with getting little bits back over such a long time? What was the catch? Why would a lender allow that? The reason was government backing meant less risk for the lender. There were more favorable terms, and more money started flowing into housing. With payments spread out for that long, you could "afford" a lot higher loan amount, leading to increased home values.

Standardized government-backed loan terms were trialed and extended again in the late 1940s to a 30-year term. It was slowly adopted until modeled by the Department of Veterans Affairs for their new 30-year home loan benefit. That loan exploded in use, made the 30-year mortgage normal, and eventually the 30-year amortization term became necessary for most people to buy homes at ever-increasing values.

It's important to understand that this is the foundation of our current housing system. This is how a mortgage requiring mandatory monthly payments for 30 years, one where we are choosing to pay a multiple of the value in total interest, became the norm. We smile and can't wait to sign! We do it because it's now become so familiar to us. We believe the property will appreciate over the time we own it to compensate for the interest.

The first recorded reverse mortgage in the United States was written in 1961 to Nellie Young of Portland, Maine. A local private banker, Nelson Haynes, wanted to help the wife of his high school football coach after her husband passed away. The loss of her husband's income meant money was tight, but she didn't want to sacrifice her cherished family home in order to make ends meet. So, Haynes got creative and designed a loan that would allow her to stay in her home and draw down the equity to pay bills and upkeep on the house. There was no magic or sorcery. He didn't create anything for her. He simply helped her convert what she already had into something she could actually use to live out her life worry-free.

The next few decades, academics and government planners in developed nations began looking at home equity release products. The forecasts in the U.S. weren't difficult to see. The boom in population from 1946 to 1964 would translate to an average of 10,000 folks hitting retirement age every day by 2008. These people would be leaving the workforce and eligible for retirement benefits, sitting on a mountain of home equity compared to the value of other liquid assets that may have been lost to inflation.

In 1983, the Consumer Price Index replaced a great housing cost indicator with a less reliable rent equivalent formula. They removed "housing" as homeowners view the cost and replaced it with "shelter," classifying the cost as a consumable. A house is accounted for by the government as Owner Equivalent Rent (OER). It's measured in part by asking people how much they could rent their house for. The takeaway here is that the government views housing as a consumable, measured for any total length of time by multiplying the OER by the time owned. Anything else related to ownership itself is not accounted for other than the rent equivalent. So, what's the point?

Not to diminish the emotion and sentiment of a house being made a home, but it's classified by the system as a consumable, so perhaps it needs to be viewed that way. Perhaps the name of the game needs to be, "How do I minimize my lifetime *shelter* cost paid?"

By the early 1980s, Congress began to more vigorously debate what a standardized home equity release product would look like with traditional defined benefit pension plans peaking in 1983 and elective defined contribution plans like 401Ks on the rise. The government created the reverse mortgage program for this exact purpose—to create a safe vehicle for converting paper gains of home equity into income tax-free cash to be a fourth rail along with personal savings, social security, and what has accumulated in retirement accounts.

Retirees lacked the borrowing ability of their working peers even though they had accumulated assets.

During those debates, reverse mortgages were described as a program that would benefit people with age-based special needs that couldn't be addressed without access to an ever-growing part of their net worth. The phrase "age discrimination" was used a lot in these congressional hearings to describe how it felt to be retired in America without proper access to your full balance sheet.

Ironically, during one of the first congressional hearings on Aging in Place and Home Equity conversions in January 1985, they discussed the risk of the program looking too good to be true and people feeling that they could never have their cake and eat it too as a risk for adoption. How right they were. And we'll discuss these and other misconceptions later in the book. But in 1987, the Housing and Community Development Act was passed:

> "The Housing and Community Development Act of 1987 (P.L. 100-242, 2/5/88) established a Federal mortgage insurance program, Section 255 of the National Housing Act, to insure home equity conversion mortgages. The program is administered by the Department of Housing and Urban Development (HUD). Pursuant to the 1987 Act, the Department was authorized to insure 2,500 HECMs. These 2,500 reservations of insurance authority were allocated among the 10 HUD Regions in proportion to each Region's share of the nation's elderly homeowners. The Regional Offices of Housing then distributed the reservations among lender applicants using a random drawing method. The Omnibus Budget Reconciliation Act of 1990 (P.L. 101-508, 11/5/90) increased the Department's insurance authority to 25,000 mortgages; accordingly, the reservation system was terminated, and all Federal Housing Administration (FHA) approved lenders are now eligible to participate in the HECM program."

In 1988, the first FHA Home Equity Conversion Mortgage was endorsed. It was the Wild West in the lending world without a lot of guardrails on what lenders could charge and how much people could take out upfront. Many needy borrowers were fleeced by greedy loan sharks all over the country. Today's retirees, in their 30s and 40s at the time, were still shaking off dust from their first bout with hyperinflation and big market crash. For years, there weren't many reverse mortgages being done.

TOTAL REVERSE MORTGAGES BY YEAR[6]

Federal year	Number of reverse mortgages	Federal year	Number of reverse mortgages
1990	157	2007	107,558
1991	389	2008	112,154
1992	1,019	2009	114,692
1993	1,964	2010	79,106
1994	3,365	2011	73,131
1995	4,165	2012	54,822
1996	3,596	2013	60,091
1997	5,208	2014	51,642
1998	7,896	2015	58,043
1999	7,982	2016	48,902
2000	6,640	2017	55,332
2001	7,781	2018	48,359
2002	13,049	2019	31,274
2003	18,097	2020	41,859
2004	37,829	2021	49,207
2005	43,131	2022	61,257
2006	76,351		
Total reverse mortgages (through October 2022)		**1,286,057**	

6. "Annual HECM Endorsement Chart" National Reverse Mortgage Lenders Association (2022). https://www.nrmlaonline.org/annual-hecm-endorsement-chart

And just when they started to gain some traction, we rolled into the year 2008. Unfortunately, many homeowners lost homes when they failed to keep up with property charges. Although the home loss had nothing to do with the product itself, it added to the reverse mortgage stigma right when the first Baby Boomer was turning 62. Around this time, nearly 10% of homeowners who took advantage of the FHA-insured reverse mortgage were in default due to their inability to pay either their property taxes, home insurance, or both. While these defaults rarely ended in foreclosure, reverse mortgages were beginning to develop a bad reputation. And the drain on insurance funds caused by costly losses wasn't so great for the government or taxpayers either.

By 2011, a couple big banks doing reverse mortgages pulled out of the market. Again, this was not because the product lacked benefit to the consumer, but because reputational headline risk of "kicking seniors out of their homes" outweighed the profit potential at the time, especially given the other issues big banks were dealing with. By law, if a property owner is delinquent on taxes, the lender must initiate a foreclosure process to get the county it's payment. The reverse mortgage has nothing to do with the legal action, yet it is coded as a "reverse mortgage foreclosure" and the bank still kicked someone out of their house. This created a negative narrative picked up by organizations looking for clickbait headlines.

Unfortunately, many people, including people in the financial sector, are unaware of the changes that came about after 2013 when Congress passed the Reverse Mortgage Stabilization Act. This piece of legislation authorized HUD to create and implement policy changes to reduce the chances of default and make the program even better.

After these policy changes, the rate of default on these loans has been lower.

The Federal Housing Commissioner at the time, Carol Galante, noted, "Our goal here is to make certain our reverse mortgage program is a financially sustainable option for seniors that will allow them to age in place in their own homes."

We've already discussed in previous chapters the two major policy changes that came about because of the Reverse Mortgage Stabilization Act of 2013. But they are worth reiterating here in context. First, the amount of home equity available to borrowers was restricted and the rate at which they could access the funds was slowed. Second, a financial assessment to evaluate a borrower's income and credit was made a requirement of the program. Along with this assessment, the Life Expectancy Set Aside (LESA) was created. If a borrower doesn't meet certain financial criteria, a LESA may be implemented, which doesn't mean someone can't qualify, but means a portion of their equity is set aside to pay for ongoing property tax and insurance.

These changes have had very positive effects on the outcomes of individual loans and the program as a whole. But many don't know these changes ever happened. Other changes include more protections for non-borrowing spouses, an insurance pricing update, changing the index adjustable rates are tied to, anti-churning provisions, and caps on fees.

As academics continue to study the applications and designs of reverse mortgages, there will certainly be more enhancements as they become much more mainstream.

REVERSE MORTGAGES IN REAL LIFE

Using a reverse mortgage to pay for the taxes incurred with a Roth Conversion is an incredibly strategic move if the future tax rate on IRA money is expected to be higher later. This was the case with Calvin. He wanted a way to create flexible retirement income while also setting up the possibility of a greater value to his estate, so his financial advisor recommended looking into this strategy.

Calvin was able to do a reverse mortgage on his paid-off home, which afforded him a $250,000 reverse line of credit. He used this to pay the tax bills on his Roth Conversion to maximize how much stayed in the tax-deferred Roth IRA for future growth. The interest he is accruing on the balance to his line of credit was 5%, while the Roth is growing long term at his investment's rate of return tax-deferred and tax-free when it comes out later. This is a powerful way for him to leverage his assets and minimize future income liability for himself or his adult children on a much bigger sum of money at a future date.

Using the reverse line of credit to pay these taxes provided Calvin with the liquidity to reallocate a portion of his net worth into a tax-free status. This created the flexibility he desired and the potential for a bigger estate down the line without leaving his children a ticking tax bomb.

— 6 —

COMMON QUESTIONS ABOUT REVERSE MORTGAGES

For many seniors, a reverse mortgage is a panacea—the solution that lets them access the wealth in their house while still calling it home.

Over the years, reverse mortgages have evolved. New regulations have been implemented by the FHA to make them one of the safest mortgage products available for consumers. But even with these safeguards in place, a reverse mortgage is still a very big decision and you and your loved ones will likely have questions. Every situation is different, and I recommend speaking independently with a loan officer, HUD counselor, and/or financial advisor to get targeted answers to your personal concerns and queries.

It's worth addressing some of the most commonly asked questions here to gain clarity about how this financial product could help you live a better life in retirement and what impact it could have on your family members. Below I'll answer common questions a potential borrower may have, as well as questions that frequently arise from spouses and heirs.

BORROWER FAQS

How much will it cost to get a reverse mortgage?

Just like with a traditional mortgage, there are fees, charges, and closing costs associated with setting up a reverse mortgage.

In addition to the interest on the loan, which accrues based on how much you use and for how long, the cost to do a reverse mortgage includes the following:

1. Upfront Mortgage Insurance Premium (MIP)

The borrower pays a fee to the FHA to receive protections from the Federal Government. This ensures that the borrower receives continuous access to their reverse mortgage proceeds if the company servicing the loan were no longer able to meet their obligations. Moreover, if the sale of a home isn't enough to pay back the loan, this insurance protects the borrower and their heirs from having to cover that loss. The cost for this upfront mortgage insurance is 2% of your maximum claim amount, which is the lesser of either the appraised value of your home or the FHA lending limit. As you can imagine, this cost is not insignificant and should be considered carefully.

2. Origination Fee

The origination fee covers a lender's operating expenses. It is how they get paid for originating—creating—the reverse mortgage. Origination fees for HECMs are capped at $6,000.

3. HUD-Approved Counseling

Before obtaining a HECM, you are required to receive counseling from an independent, HUD-approved counselor. The charge for the counseling tends to be between $150-300. HUD maintains a list on their website of all certified counselors in the country so consumers can shop around. It is always worth asking the agency if they have any grants or discounts available for the session.

Other Closing Costs

Other closing costs that could be incurred include the following:

- **Recording Fee** – To record the mortgage lien at the County Recorder's Office, a borrower may pay between $0-250, subject to their location.

- **Credit Report Fee** – The borrow pays a fee for the lender to obtain their credit report, usually $25-100.
- **Survey** – A survey may be requested to determine if any adjoining properties have encroached on the borrower's property or vice versa, and usually costs $200-2000.
- **Title/Escrow Fees** – Title companies will typically charge flat rates for their title and escrow services, which may be broken out separately or itemized, and usually cost $300-1000.
- **Title Insurance** – The borrower will need to pay for title insurance to protect themselves as well as the lender from problems that may arise with the home's title, such as back taxes or liens on the house. Title insurance typically costs $200-1000.
- **Appraisal Fees** – The appraiser of the house charges a fee for their services, usually between $650-1000, depending on the complexity of the property and market in your area.

Possible Additional Costs

- **Repair Set-Aside** (dictated by appraiser before closing) – Because this is a federal program, your home must meet federal regulations for structural integrity, local building codes, and safety. During a home appraisal, if the appraiser decides the property is not up to code, the borrower will need to make the necessary repairs to move forward with the mortgage. If these repairs are valued at less than 15% of the maximum claim amount, a repair set-aside can be established from the reverse mortgage proceeds in order to make the repairs. Otherwise, you will have to account for the expense of any needed repairs before you can get a reverse mortgage.
- **Liens and Federal Debt** (dictated by credit history) – If a borrower has any liens on their property, these must also be paid off at closing. A reverse mortgage is a first position lien,

meaning the reverse mortgage is first in line to the value of the home, so if you have any other debt where the home is used as collateral, that debt must be paid off. Federal debt must also be taken care of with the reverse mortgage proceeds. If you still owe money on your traditional mortgage, you'll have to pay it off at the closing of the reverse mortgage. So if you qualified for a $250,000 reverse mortgage but still owed $200,000 on your home, you would be left with $50,000. For some homeowners, this may not be worth the amount of money they'd gain, but for many, getting that traditional mortgage payment off their back alone is a blessing.

Hypothetical Closing Costs Example

Finance Charges	**Paid Outside Closing**	**Estimated Amount**
Origination fee		$4,000
Flood certification		$18
Document preparation		$160
Property Tax Verification fee		$100
Repair administration		$100
4506-C Direct/IRS		$50
Attorney Review Fee		$350
Mortgage Insurance Premium		$12,000
Settlement or closing fee		$615
Counseling fee	$175	$0
Other Charges		
Appraisal fee	$650	$0
Credit report		$35
Lender's title insurance		$580
Recording charges mortgage		$100
	$825	$18,108
Total Estimated Settlement Costs		$18,933

As you can see, with the insurance included, there can be some significant costs to a reverse mortgage, which is part of why it's so important to work with reputable lenders and loan officers. And there may be expenses not listed here. Like anything else, it's important to consider the cost benefit of obtaining a reverse mortgage when considering whether it's the best option for you.

When will I have to pay back the loan?

Unlike a forward mortgage, reverse mortgages don't have a specified end date until the last borrower turns 150 years old. Instead, they become due and payable when the last borrower moves out of the home or passes away. However, there are instances when the loan may need to be paid back sooner. This could happen if the home is no longer be your principal residence, you have failed to pay taxes and insurance, or the home has not been maintained. These are what are known as "maturity events," occurrences in which the loan will become due.

A HECM must be paid off when the last surviving borrower or eligible non-borrowing spouse meets one of these requirements:

- Sells the property
- Dies
- Is away from the home for 12 consecutive months
- Fails to meet borrower responsibilities (taxes, homeowner's insurance, property maintenance)

Failure to meet borrower responsibilities can put your loan in default. At that time, if you're unable to pay the mortgage balance, the mortgage company can foreclose and sell your property.

It's important to consider the possibility of these events. If something happens that may cause the loan to become due prior to when you had planned, you should have a plan in place. Communicating with the servicer, monitoring your monthly statements, checking your mail, and certifying HUD annual occupancy letters are critical.

What are the benefits of a reverse mortgage line of credit (LOC)?

An adjustable-rate reverse mortgage offers flexibility that allows you to choose how you want to receive your funds. This includes the option of taking an initial amount but leaving the remaining funds to access as-needed in a line of credit (LOC), or taking no money upfront and leaving all of it to access as-needed. There are a couple features of this LOC that make it worth considering.

First, the HECM LOC is federally insured, so it can never be closed or frozen by the lender while you have funds available, and you don't have interest accrue on those funds until you use them.

Second, the unused portion of a HECM LOC grows at the same rate as the loan accrues interest (plus mortgage insurance premium). That means the amount of money available to you through your line of credit tends to gets larger over time if you don't pull from it. While investments will go up and down depending on whether we're in a bull or bear market, this line of credit has a guaranteed growth rate. It will continue to grow regardless of economic outlook and future home values.

For example, if your interest is 3.25% and your mortgage insurance premium (MIP) is 0.5%, you are looking at an accrual rate of 3.75%. So if you had a credit line of $250,000, it would grow by $781.25 in the first month, and continue to grow from there ($250,000 x 3.75%/12 months). Each month, you'd have more money available to you should you need it, and it continues to grow based on that new, larger balance each month. Many people who choose to set up a line of credit don't need to use the money right away, and it gives them peace of mind knowing the funds are there if they ever need them.

Line of Credit Example

Beginning mortgage balance: $18,108

Expected interest rate: 5.390%

Initial property value: $600,000

Maximum claim amount: $600,000

Initial principal limit: $309,600

Initial advance: $0

Expected appreciation: 4%

Monthly disbursement: $0

Initial line of credit: $291,492

Product type: 1 year CMT

Financed closing cost: $18,108

Year	Age	MIP	Interest	Loan Balance	Line of Credit	Principal Limit	Property Value	Equity
0	80	0	0	18,108	291,492	309,600	600,000	581,892
1	81	93	1,003	19,204	309,132	328,336	624,000	604,796
2	82	99	1,063	20,366	327,840	348,206	648,960	628,594
3	83	105	1,128	21,598	347,679	369,278	674,918	653,320
4	84	125	1,196	22,906	368,720	391,625	701,915	679,009
5	85	118	1,268	24,292	391,033	415,325	729,992	705,700
10	90	158	1,702	32,587	524,566	557,153	888,147	855,560
15	95	212	2,283	43,715	703,699	747,415	1,080,566	1,036,851
20	100	284	3,062	58,643	944,005	1,002,648	1,314,674	1,256,031

Couldn't I just sell my property, move to a rental, and use the proceeds from the sale as cash flow?

Sure. Reverse mortgages offer a solution for people who have a desire to stay in their home for as long as possible. That yearning to remain in the family home was what prompted Nelson Haynes to write the very first reverse mortgage. If staying in your home is not your ultimate goal, then there are other ways to access the equity in your home. Selling is another way to liquidate that asset.

However, academic research from gerontologists and human ecologists looking at ways to improve aging note that the $9 trillion of home equity that exists amongst our over-62 population could be better used. Do people over 62 sell their homes and rent because they want to, or because they didn't know all their options? I believe that all too often it's the latter.

Reverse Mortgage vs. Renting

In some parts of the country, selling and renting could be a great option. If you don't prefer to stay in your home long term, and rent rates are relatively low in your area, selling your home will give you access to the cash you need. However, this isn't always the case. My mom is a perfect example. Rents are incredibly high where she lives. When she was weighing her options recently between buying a new home and renting, she found that even with HOA fees, the housing cost for buying was considerably lower than renting. For her, renting didn't make sense. It made sense to buy and lock in a housing cost that wouldn't go up with a landlord's house value.

Selling a home outright allows you to access your equity but can also cause major disruptions in life, as you must navigate a move and a new residence. It also includes all the costs associated with moving as well as rental expenses that are not fixed and likely much higher than a mortgage payment in a comparable property.

Another way to access a home's equity is through a forward loan or line of credit. But these options require monthly principle and interest payments that could affect your cash flow, and you have to qualify for them with full underwriting. Many times, these recurring payments are what lead seniors to continue working part-time or even full-time after retirement age. They simply can't make the budget work without some sort of income. Eliminating monthly payments is a huge benefit of a reverse mortgage, offering many a freedom they never knew possible.

Reverse mortgage products are the only option that allows you to access equity while also staying in the home so you can maximize retirement on your own terms—no disruptive moves, no monthly payments, and all backed by the FHA.

NON-BORROWING SPOUSE FAQS

What happens if my spouse passes away before me?

In 2014, HUD added provisions to protect non-borrowing spouses who outlive their borrowing spouse.

Prior to these changes, if a person was not on the loan, they were not protected. After their borrowing spouse passed away, the loan became due, and often the house would need to be sold in a certain amount of time to pay it off especially if there weren't other assets available to pay it off from the estate. If the non-borrowing spouse wanted to stay in the home, they would have to do one of the following:

1. If they were over 62, they could refinance it by doing their own reverse mortgage, assuming they had enough equity.

2. More commonly, they could refinance into a forward mortgage on the remaining balance (back to making monthly payments).
3. They could sell and find a new place to live.

This final option is the one that left many non-borrowing spouses feeling like they'd been kicked out of their home. They simply didn't have the assets to pay the debt off without the house itself. It led to a lot of heartbreak. Thankfully, the loan terms have changed, and eligible non-borrowing spouses are protected.

After the updates, a non-borrowing spouse can stay in the home without disruption until the time a maturity event occurs. Even if they're under 62, they can retain the right to stay in the house after their spouse passes away if they continue to pay property taxes, insurance, and HOA fees and maintain the home as their primary residence.

To allow for this change, the non-borrowing spouse now factors into the equation when the lender provides the borrower with a Principal Loan Limit (PLL). The new provisions dictate that the PLL is based on the youngest borrower *or* the youngest eligible non-borrowing spouse. The loan will not be considered due until the non-borrowing spouse sells the home or passes away.

Ineligible Non-Borrowing Spouse

A non-borrowing spouse whose primary residence is *not* the property with the reverse mortgage in question would be considered ineligible and would not qualify for non-borrowing spouse protections. This might be the case if a non-borrowing spouse lives in a nursing home or full-time assisted living facility. Additionally, if a couple's marriage occurred after the loan was started, the non-borrowing spouse would also be considered ineligible.

Will I still receive payments or have access to the line of credit after my spouse dies?

Unfortunately, no. The protections to the non-borrowing spouse only allow for you to stay in the home as long as you like and to defer payment of the loan until another maturity event occurs.

Loan disbursement payments and access to remaining funds in the line of credit will cease after the death of the borrower. The loan continues to accrue interest and the monthly Mortgage Insurance Premium must continue to be paid for the life of the loan. These are obligations that a loan officer will go over with both the borrowing and non-borrowing spouse during the application process.

HEIR FAQS

Will I be responsible if there is a loss on the sale of the house?

No. One of the greatest benefits of the FHA-insured reverse mortgage is that it is non-recourse. This means that borrowers can never owe more than the appraised value of the home at the time the loan is due, even if the loan balance is higher than that appraised value. No one can be on the hook for that difference, including heirs.

Typically, heirs simply sell the house and keep the difference if there are remaining proceeds after the reverse mortgage balance has been paid off.

The estate has a HUD-standard 180 days to settle once the last person, whether borrower or protected non-borrowing spouse, passes, but technically at this point the loan becomes due and can generate scary letters from the servicer. So, first and foremost, the person assigned as the legal representation of the estate needs to notify the servicer as soon as possible so they can help you to understand all your options.

The person needs to have current proof of authority or the servicer will not discuss it. The servicer can grant extensions for repayment beyond 30 days, but only through constant update and communication with them.

In most cases, the house is now owned by the estate or named beneficiaries. However, there is a mortgage that is due and there are a few ways you can handle this.

Even if the loan balance is higher than the appraised value of the home, the estate can simply send the keys to the FHA and wipe their hands of it. The house pays for the debt and the FHA insurance protects you against possible losses.

If you want to buy the house, you could purchase it from the estate at this point. You would be paying the appraised value of the home and would either pay cash or finance it on your own. You would be buying it in the same way you would if it were anyone else's house. If you already lived in the home of the borrower and you want to purchase it, there may be limitations, so make sure to discuss with your loan officer or servicer.

If you've inherited the house, the loan is still considered payable within 30 days. With servicer-approved extensions, you could have up to a year to make final decisions on how you will pay. Because you own the title, you have the option to sell the home, pay off the loan, and keep any difference. Or, if you want to keep the inherited home, you can pay off the reverse mortgage with other assets.

So, I can keep the house if I want it?

Absolutely. One of the most common myths I see about reverse mortgages is that the bank takes the title. And that's just not true.

Each state is different in how they handle titles specifically. But, in general, the person who has the title owns the home. When the reverse mortgage borrower dies, the bank does not own the title and they do not own the home. There is, however, a lien on the home that you must deal with if you want to keep the home.

Similarly, if your parent passed away with a forward mortgage on their home and you wanted to keep that home, you would have to refinance it in your own name or buy the home outright. The same is true of reverse mortgages.

If you want to keep the house in the family, the servicer will allow ample time for you to determine the best way forward. You simply need to communicate with the servicer immediately after the maturity event and let them know your interest as soon as possible to get the ball rolling.

BUYER BEWARE: RED FLAGS TO WATCH OUT FOR IN REVERSE MORTGAGES

Regardless of the updates put into effect after the implementation of the Reverse Mortgage Stabilization Act in 2013 and beyond, there are still some red flags to watch out for when you're looking for folks to work with as you put a reserve mortgage in place. Here are my top tips to borrowers that will help you avoid red flags:

Consult a planner.

Always be realistic about your own limitations. Consider your own financial literacy and how much information you may require to make an informed decision. If you have concerns, talk to a financial advisor or planner. A $250 fee for a one-hour consultation is money well spent if it will make you comfortable enough to make a decision. If your planner doesn't know about reverse mortgages, tell them you need them to get educated on it to help you make that decision. Remember, they are there to serve *you*. Most will have no problem doing additional research and reading if it means they can more expertly speak to your specific situation.

Evaluate multiple loan offers.

You should always consider getting a second opinion and look at multiple offers. Be very clear and transparent with your loan officer about what your ultimate goals are for this money. If they don't ask you questions about your goals, that's a red flag and may indicate they just want to do the loan for their own gain and may not care about how the loan will help you. To help you find a good loan officer, you can always ask for referrals from people you trust.

Consider future servicing needs.

Reverse mortgages are longer-term loans, and there are going to be questions that come up down the line, either on your end or from your family members or heirs. Work with a loan officer you know will be there to answer those questions. Personally, I tell all my reverse mortgage clients to put my business card with the paperwork in their safe. That way, if something happens to them, whoever finds the card will know to call the person or company who set up their reverse mortgage.

Counseling is there for a reason.

Listen to your HUD-approved counselor. They are a part of this process for a reason. Go in with an open mind, and don't let your loan officer "coach" you through what the conversation with your counselor is going to look like. This is another red flag that would indicate your loan officer may not have your best interest at heart. Independently consulting with your loan officer, financial planner, and HUD counselor will insure you make the best decisions to meet your financial goals.

REVERSE MORTGAGES IN REAL LIFE

Donald Stone was worried about the possibility of his health declining in the future. Without long-term care insurance and with a history of Alzheimer's in his family, he wanted a solution that would allow him the option to access funds if he ended up needing to finance potential care costs.

With a reverse mortgage, he was able to lock in the current real estate values and set up a line of credit before there was an immediate need.

His home had an appraised value of $600,000. Using the adjustable-rate option, he chose to put $200,000 in the reverse line of credit.

Now he's letting that amount grow based on what the FHA allows. Even if he doesn't need to use it anytime soon, that line of credit will continue to grow every year until it's needed. Because he's not touching the balance, his line of credit grows at the same rate that his loan accrues interest.

Because Donald set the loan up as soon as he was eligible, the line of credit will be much larger in the event that he needs to fund full-time medical care, even if housing values drop in the future.

— 7 —

CREATIVE STRATEGIES TO MAXIMIZE YOUR RETIREMENT USING A REVERSE MORTGAGE

In the wake of COVID-19, the United States has gone through major economic changes. While many groups have been affected negatively, it's put a particular type of stress on seniors. Retirees have had to return to work and soon-to-retire individuals have had to alter their plans and delay their long-awaited freedom.

With this economic shift, I noticed a rise in clients asking their advisors how they could evaluate their full balance sheets to meet their goals now. Their focus, more than ever, is on the present. A situation as dramatic as the pandemic has made many people realize that there's no predicting what tomorrow will bring.

Ask any financial advisor with their finger on the pulse, and they'll likely tell you that they've heard more clients saying something like, "We used to want to leave the house for the kids. But after a year like the one we just lived through, we've realized how short life can be. What can we do to get the most out of our retirement?"

Unfortunately, many advisors often reply, "You need to cut your spending or you're going to run out of money," or "You have to think about selling your house."

For many people in the current economic situation, pressure is building. Something's going to give. The only next logical option is to unlock the house—using it better and smarter. That's what advisors need to be telling their clients.

I believe reverse mortgages will be a huge part of the next iteration of holistic financial planning.

We can't just rely on modern portfolio theory and stocks, bonds, and cash like we've thought for the past 20 years. Now we need to incorporate home equity as well.

I want to be part of the spark. I want to be a match in the tinder. We need to evolve the industry that is ignoring one of the dearest assets a person can have—their house.

FULL BALANCE SHEET FINANCIAL PLANNING

What is a full balance sheet? Businesses often evaluate their full balance sheet when determining their financial health. The balance sheet displays their total assets and how each of these assets is financed, either with debt or with equity. Essentially, the balance sheet solves for your net worth with the following equation:

Assets – Liabilities = Equity

Your full balance sheet provides a snapshot of your personal assets and liabilities at a single point in time. It will show you what you own and how much it's worth, what debts you have, and your net worth. It can illustrate whether you're on the right trajectory to meet your financial goals.

As such, full balance sheet financial planning helps you create strategies that cover all the individual pieces of your financial puzzle and how they fit together. This sort of approach can put you in a better place to achieve your goals in realistic ways. It allows you to evaluate all those pieces to determine how they can best be used. What puzzle piece needs to be moved so that everything locks into place?

Let's discuss some strategies using the house as a primary piece of the overall financial puzzle. Every financial picture is different, and consulting with a professional about how these strategies could best be implemented to meet your own goals is critical. There's no one-size-fits-all solution. These are simply ideas I've seen work well for some people that may spark an idea for you about how to reach your own financial goals.

ACCESS TO LIQUIDITY

Reverse mortgages allow you to create liquidity through a relatively low-cost loan on what's generally considered to be an appreciating asset. This liquidity can be used strategically as part of an overall plan by using it to pay a tax liability or to avoid selling off well-performing stocks. When you assess your full balance sheet, you may find new ways of using your home equity.

A Word on Tax Diversification

Financial professionals who have your best interest in mind are always key to a strong financial plan, and having a good CPA or tax advisor is critical if you want to use a reverse mortgage as part of an overall tax strategy. Strategize with these professionals about what the tax benefits look like for your specific situation. With every strategy there are unseen risks. Very rarely does one strategy work in a vacuum. If your CPA or tax advisor does not know reverse mortgages well, ask them to get up to speed.

Proceeds from a reverse mortgage loan are not taxed as income and are considered loan proceeds by the IRS. While these funds are considered income tax-free, it's not a completely tax-free process, of course. For example, somewhere along the line you may pay a type of tax, like a transfer tax on the closing documents. You're also still responsible for property taxes. But the funds from the loan itself are not taxed as income. This provides an additional dimension on your balance sheet, which many people overlook.

Because we have a progressive tax system, higher levels of income are taxed at higher percentages. This means that someone in a top tax bracket in a state with high taxes, such as in California, could very easily be looking at a marginal tax bracket of over 50%.

Marginal tax is the rate you owe on any income above the previous tax bracket. So, when you need to access any amount pushing you into a higher tax bracket, you should carefully comb your full balance sheet. What's the most logical place for that money to come from with the lowest tax impact?

Similarly, anyone who is 72 or older and has pre-tax money put into a traditional IRA or an employer sponsored plan must start taking some of that money out in what is known as required minimum distributions (or RMDs). Someone who is 68 now and has a good amount of money in their IRA knows that a sizable tax bill is just four years away when they have to begin taking RMDs. They may need access to money that's not going to have tax implications. But where can they pull from? Again, this is where evaluating the full balance sheet can be a huge win for some people.

A reverse mortgage gives access to the money people are looking for. It's a way to convert otherwise illiquid home equity into a liquid asset. Taxes may make it more expensive to pull from other places. In that instance, tax diversification is the name of the game.

Making a Roth Conversion Work

A very common strategy is what's called a Roth Conversion. This is when you move money from a traditional IRA account into a Roth IRA account. Basically, you take future known taxable income, pay today's taxes on it, and convert it to a Roth IRA, where it will grow tax-free for the rest of your life and pass on tax-free as well. This strategy has huge advantages.

The issue is that the more you take out in today's dollars, the higher you push yourself up in today's marginal tax brackets.

For example, let's say you have $100,000 in your 401K and you want to convert it to a Roth. Your taxable income is $50,000 and you're in a 12% marginal tax bracket. Every dollar you earn up until $80,250 is all taxed at that 12%. But that next dollar—at $80,251—is going to be taxed at 22%. The conversion will to push you up into that bracket because now your taxable income for the year is $150,000. You're looking at a tax bill of $18,000, and it usually shouldn't be withheld from the 401K money, because that needs to get converted.

To make this conversion work mathematically, you need to pay those taxes from another source. Where do you get that money from? What if you don't have that cash already sitting in your account? What if you do have it, but it's locked up?

Well, again, you can look at your full balance sheet. Some people find that accessing their home equity through a reverse mortgage is a practical choice for making the Roth Conversion work. For others, the cost of the loan doesn't make sense.

But consider how this could scale. Higher net-worth individuals who implement this strategy may be looking at a tax bill of, say, $350,000 to convert $1,000,000 in today's dollars. If they have paid off their $800,000 home, depending on loan rates and their age, they may have a sizable pot to pull from with a reverse mortgage. While they've borrowed from Peter to pay Paul, they are paying less in future income taxes, which may be higher later.

This isn't a tax avoidance strategy—it is simply determining which funds make the most sense and gaining access to those funds. For some people, the house is a primary asset and those are the funds that make the most sense.

Avoiding Selling Highly Appreciated Stocks

Reverse mortgages also allow access to funds when you have highly appreciated assets that you don't want to sell (and pay tax on).

When I was in San Diego, I can't tell you how many people I knew who were early investors in large tech companies. It wasn't uncommon to see clients who had millions and millions of dollars in Apple that they had bought in at $10-20 a share. They may have put in $20,000 and it was now worth $2 million. Since 2010, this phenomenon isn't limited to Silicon Valley. There are people all over the country invested in Facebook, Amazon, Netflix, Microsoft, Pfizer—mega cap companies that haven't gone down and are trading at 100 times earnings. A lot of people have highly appreciated stock and they're reticent about selling.

When you sell stocks for a profit, you are subject to capital gains tax. As it stands, capital gains tax is lower than ordinary income tax, but it's still 15% in higher brackets, or 20% for someone who is in the highest bracket. Some states tax it too.

In a scenario where someone needs access to liquidity, one of their options is to sell a highly appreciated stock, incurring capital gains tax along the way. Instead, they might decide, "I know my Apple stock is worth 2 million. But if I sell it right now to get the funds I need for something else, I'm going to get crushed with taxes. I'll tap into the liquidity in my house instead." They can then use a reverse mortgage to avoid selling all those stocks at once and still gain the liquidity they need from their assets. Maybe they sell later when they have an offsetting loss or are in a lower tax bracket.

Reverse Mortgage vs. Borrowing Against Your Portfolio

If you need access to money, one option I hear many suggest is to borrow against your portfolio—also known as a margin loan. However, that collateral isn't as rock-solid to your lender as a house and the terms aren't as favorable.

The cost to borrow against your portfolio is called a margin rate. The margin rate at one popular financial services company at the time of writing is 9.575% if you want to borrow $250k-500k; 10% for $50k-249k; and over 11.3% for anything less than $25k. You have to pay this premium rate to create the liquidity you need.

The other issue is that that your portfolio is marked-to-market every day. While you can borrow a percentage, you're beholden to the market. If your portfolio is a million dollars and you're able to borrow $250,000 one day, the stock market could drop the next day and then your portfolio is only worth $900,000. In that case, you may have to immediately add more money. And if you don't pay, you're going to be forced to start selling pieces of that portfolio off. The house, on the other hand, is stable collateral. You always know what the rate is, and with a HECM, you'll never be responsible for more than the house with worth.

APPRECIATION ON MULTIPLE HOMES

If purchasing a second home is one of your goals in retirement, it can be extremely beneficial to consider the equity you already have in your first home as part of your strategy, essentially borrowing from one house to buy another house.

Why would you do this? The alternative could be getting another forward mortgage to borrow more money, probably paying similar interest rates to the reverse, but the property value could drop, and your heirs could be underwater. With a reverse mortgage, you're never on the hook for more than the house is valued.

Let's look at a couple, both 70 years old, who own their $800,000 home outright. They could maintain that home as their primary residence and receive $400,000 through a reverse mortgage and use that money to pay for a second home in cash, maybe even making their offer stronger to get a lower price.

On an annual basis they have property taxes, insurance, and HOA fees for two homes. But now they have a 1.2-million-dollar real estate portfolio, leveraged at just $400,000.

Even if you ignore those numbers, think about the benefit to this family's lives. Can you really put a price tag on that cabin the whole family can use for the last 20 or 30 years of your life? I don't think you can.

The linchpin here is that they own that second house free and clear, and the loan they used is non-recourse. Their other assets are protected. They're protected on the interest rate on the upside, but also protected on the downside as well if house values drop.

A "Put" on Your House

In stock trading, there are what's called "calls" and "puts." A "call" is an option to buy something at a certain price. A "put" is an option to sell something at a certain price. Placing a put on something means you can never sell it for less, even if the value drops. A reverse mortgage effectively works as a put on your house. You can borrow based on this locked-in higher amount, and even if the value drops later, it doesn't matter. The put protects your ability to borrow off that higher value.

CHARITABLE GIVING

Let's say you want to give a large gift to charity, and you'd rather do it while you're alive so you can see the benefits for yourself. If you're worried about giving other liquid assets because there's always a chance you may need to tap them later for care or unforeseen costs, you still have access to your home equity and plan to stay in your home.

Consider someone without heirs who has a much-loved nonprofit as their beneficiary. They may have considered leaving their house to this group, but that would be a gift after life. There's no financial benefit to the giver and they won't get as much emotional benefit as if they could see the fruits of their gift. If they wanted to realize the gift sooner and determined that the cost of doing it made sense, they could use a reverse mortgage to access the money in the house and give the gift now.

If a 70-year-old widow in this situation wanted to make a gift to her former high school, she could use a reverse mortgage to do that. Perhaps she was once a well-known track star, and the school offered to name their track after her providing she made a gift of $200,000. I don't know about you, but I'd certainly consider that! If she had a home worth $400,000, paid off, it would be possible for her to make that gift with a reverse mortgage.

Now, this isn't free money. It's money that needs to be evaluated against all the other alternatives. In the case of our track star, maybe there was no other money available, but this gift was a major life goal for her. Maybe she had ample other assets available to gift, but planned to stay in the home a long time anyway and didn't want to deplete the existing liquid assets too far. Thanks to the reverse mortgage, she can now look forward to 20 years of attending events and seeing her name in lights.

SETTING UP A LINE OF CREDIT EARLY

You are eligible for a reverse mortgage as soon as you turn 62, and there's a growing number of advisors who will tell you that this is the optimal time to do one—as soon as possible. This way, if something unforeseen occurs, you can draw on your line of credit. When the housing bubble burst back in 2008, many HELOCs were closed or frozen. It's happening now, during the writing of this book, as property values are softening and layoffs increase. This won't happen with reverse mortgage lines of credit, as long as you maintain your borrower obligations.

Right now, home values are at all-time highs so locking in makes sense. But there's an even more compelling reason to set up a line of credit early. When you need the money, you can use it. You don't have to pay it back until you leave the home.

As with all strategies that involve a reverse mortgage, the benefit here is contingent upon a plan to stay in your home long enough to reap the benefits over any costs. Because the up-front cost to set up a reverse mortgage is higher than, say, a home equity line of credit, this is an important factor to consider.

REVERSE MORTGAGES IN REAL LIFE

Divorce is pretty common in older individuals and is often referred to as "silver divorce." In fact, according to the U.S. Census Bureau, divorce rates are highest among individuals between 55 and 64 years old.

Leon and Karla decided to get a divorce at 65 years old. At this point in their lives, they truly had to split their household, including both assets and income. But they had one big asset worth $600,000: their house.

Typically, in this situation, the wife may want to stay in the house as long as possible and the husband says, "Okay, I'll go find my own place." But, of course, it happens both ways. In this scenario, the person who stays in the house has to "buy out" the other spouse. They end up selling off other assets to come up with the money or giving more stuff to the other spouse to pay for their half. The person leaving gets the cash amount that their half of the house is worth. In this instance, they agreed Karla would stay in the house, so she needed to come up with $300,000 to give to Leon.

Because Karla didn't have $300,000 to give him, they worried they might have to sell the house. They thought that was the only fair way—nobody would get the house, and they would split the net of fees. Perhaps they would each get $275,000 after the sale and go off to do their own thing. But then they would have to qualify for their own loans and pay monthly mortgage payments.

Instead, they learned they could do a reverse mortgage, which would allow Karla, as the borrower, to get out half the equity and cut the check to Leon. She'd need to maintain property taxes and general upkeep of the home, but she'd also get any future appreciation.

To take it one step further, Leon decided to use that $300,000 as a down payment and did a HECM for Purchase on another $600,000 house. They both got a house of equal value, and nobody had to pay out of other liquid assets for a single thing.

Whether you're an estate planner, a divorce attorney, or a couple going through a silver divorce of your own, there are options out there. The old way is the inefficient way.

Karla had an emotional attachment to the home she'd lived in most of her adult life, but she lacked the cash to hold on to it. Finding wealth in that very house meant she was able to stay put, and neither she nor Leon had to pull money out of retirement accounts to create the new living situations they both enjoy.

— 8 —

A QUICK REFERENCE GUIDE TO REVERSE MORTGAGES

We've covered a lot of information, so let's do a quick recap to help you remember the most important details. You can use this chapter as a reference guide, a reminder, or a resource to show your family and friends who have questions about reverse mortgages.

WHAT IS A REVERSE MORTGAGE, AND WHY WOULD YOU WANT TO DO ONE?

A reverse mortgage is a loan that allows to you draw from the equity you have in your home. Similar to a traditional mortgage, it uses the home as collateral. However, instead of making monthly principle and interest payments, you aren't required to pay any of the loan back as long as you live in the home and continue to meet the obligations of the loan, which include maintaining the property and paying property taxes, although interest still accrues to the balance during this time.

When the loan becomes due, either because you move out, pass away, or another "maturity event" occurs (see page 99 for specifics about maturity events), you have several options for paying back the loan, but in most cases, the value of the house pays for the loan. Usually, borrowers choose to sell the house, and the remaining money after repaying the loan can be pocketed. Because houses tend to appreciate, it is rare for a home to "go under" and be unable to pay off the loan, but even if that is the case, you cannot be held accountable for more than the house is worth at the time the loan is due, because reverse mortgages are non-recourse loans and insured by the FHA.

Reverse mortgages are a loan product designed specifically for seniors in order to help increase their quality of life during retirement. Many retirees have most of their wealth tied up in their home. This can lead to financial challenges such as having to work longer than you'd like in order to maintain the income you need, or being unable to pursue your dreams for retirement because you don't have the financial means. A reverse mortgage can allow you to live a more comfortable life and focus on what matters most to you by providing the money you need to design your own retirement. It could be as simple as paying off the rest of your mortgage so you don't have monthly payments over your head, or as big as taking the trip around the world you've always dreamed of. You've already built the wealth in your house, and a reverse mortgage allows you to access it and take advantage of that, flipping the switch from accumulation to decumulation on your entire balance sheet. Reverse mortgages can also be used as part of a strategic financial plan, such as to purchase another home, minimize your tax burden, or even get rid of a traditional mortgage payment.

Here is an easy acronym I came up with that highlights the list of top reverse mortgage financial planning opportunities:

(P)urchase a retirement home with a fraction down and keep the difference in the bank/portfolio

(A)void marginal tax bracket creep and Medicare increases on high-spend years

(R)oth conversion tax liability funding

(K)eep the home you love, but upgrade or modify for age-in-place renovations

(E)xisting mortgage payoff or refinance to eliminate debt payment and free up cash flow

(R)eLOC (Reverse Line of Credit) bridge for longevity planning, in-home care funding, supplementing your portfolio in down years to mitigate sequence of returns risk, or avoiding low basis sales to fund big purchases like vacations or cars

WHAT DO YOU NEED TO QUALIFY FOR A REVERSE MORTGAGE?

- At least one of the borrowers must be 62 years old or older.
- You must generally have at least 50-70% equity in your home.
- The home must be your primary residence, meaning you live there at least 183 days out of the year.
- You should not be delinquent on any federal debt (exceptions may apply).
- You must participate in an independent consumer education session with an HUD-approved reverse mortgage counselor.

TYPES OF REVERSE MORTGAGES

HECM versus Private Reverse Mortgage

A home equity conversion mortgage (HECM) is an FHA-insured reverse mortgage, which is non-recourse, meaning that no one can be held responsible for the loan if the value of the house drops and the loan cannot be paid off through the sale of the house. For this reason, HECMs are the most secure type of reverse mortgage and are what most borrowers will want.

There are also private reverse mortgages that are not insured by the FHA. Usually if you're looking at a private loan, it's because you want to borrow more than the FHA lending limit. These are called jumbo loans and require you to go through a private lender.

HECM Payout Options

With a HECM, you have multiple options for how you may structure your loan and receive money, depending on how you intend to use it. You can choose to receive the proceeds upfront, in dispersed payments, as a line of credit, or in a combination of various methods. The money you receive is not taxed as income, and you don't have to pay it off until you leave the house or another maturity event occurs.

- **Lump Sum** – You receive all funds upfront and it's up to you to determine how to use that money.
- **Partial Lump Sum** – You receive a portion of your available sums and then choose a secondary payment option for the remainder.
- **Tenure** – You receive all funds in fixed monthly payments for the entire life of the loan.

- **Modified Tenure** – You receive a lower fixed monthly payment, and the difference goes into a line of credit for the entire life of the loan.
- **Term** – You receive fixed monthly payments for a fixed period of months rather than the life of the loan.
- **Modified Term** – You receive fixed monthly payments for a fixed period of months and a line of credit for the entire life of the loan.
- **Line of Credit** – Your funds are available upon request, and the balance grows at the same rate as the loan's interest, so your available funds increase over time as long as you don't withdraw from the line of credit.

HECM for Purchase

A HECM for purchase is very similar to a regular home-financing purchase loan, but it is structured differently. If you want to buy a new home rather than staying in your current home, this may be the right option for you. Like a traditional mortgage, you borrow money to purchase the home, but with a HECM for purchase, you won't have a monthly mortgage payment. You must still pay property taxes and insurance as well as maintain the property.

IS A REVERSE MORTGAGE RIGHT FOR YOU?

Reverse mortgages can be extremely beneficial to many retirees. If you want to stay in your home, it's a great way to access the equity you've built without having to sell your home in order to rent or downsize.

Here are three common scenarios in which a reverse mortgage is a great solution:

1. Your mortgage is fully paid off and you want to access the wealth you've built in its equity for another purpose.

2. You're still making payments on your mortgage or some other kind of lien on your house and would like to remove the burden of those payments.
3. You have a strategic financial plan that the proceeds from a reverse mortgage can help you achieve.

Reverse mortgages aren't only for people who are strapped for cash. While it can be a major benefit to someone who doesn't have the income they need to maintain their lifestyle, it can also be beneficial to someone who has a significant amount of wealth as part of a larger financial plan. You can learn more about various creative strategies for reverse mortgages in chapter 6.

The most important thing to do when considering a reverse mortgage is to look at your finances as a whole with full balance sheet financial planning. Talk to a financial advisor and carefully consider your reasons for looking into a reverse mortgage. I recommend writing down why you want a reverse mortgage as soon as you begin thinking about it so you don't lose track of your goal and are able to keep the purpose in mind to avoid making choices that don't benefit that purpose. While a reverse mortgage can be beneficial, there are costs involved in attaining one, and it's a decision that should be made from a place where you feel informed and confident.

REVERSE MORTGAGES IN REAL LIFE

Could you imagine making it through life by age 62 and someone says you can only use a *portion* of the money you were able to save and accumulate? That is how it feels for many retirees who may have a large part of their wealth tied up in their house.

Net worth is defined as the value of all assets, minus the total of all liabilities. So, let's consider Sue with a net worth of $1,000,000 in her early 70s. Her home accounts for $700,000 and her liquid assets $300,000. Her advisor tells her if she wants to stay in her house, she can responsibly spend approximately 4-5% of her liquid assets. That's $12,000-$15,000! Effectively, Sue is a millionaire pinching pennies on only $1,000-$1,250 a month on top of her social security.

It simply isn't fair to tell Sue her only option is to spend less, move, or add more risk to her life with an additional monthly payment, because it's not true. There is a solution the Federal Government created for any qualifying homeowner 62 or older, regardless of net worth, for this exact purpose. It's right in front of our faces.

Once Sue got to retirement, she realized she wasn't given great advice on how to best prepare for retirement, because she's now in a bit of a pinch and shouldn't be when her assets are worth $1,000,000. Additionally, the $300,000 in investments she was counting on growing early in retirement has been hit hard and she's compelled to go to cash to at least preserve a few good years in her home, but deep down she knows she'll fall further behind if she does that.

What if Sue could magically convert some of that home value to liquid assets? Technically it would be the same long-term outcome if managed properly, but in this case, she can now live off $28,000-$35,000 a year, stay in the family home, and feel much more at peace. She would have $2,300-$2,900 to spend monthly on top of her social security and small pension. Except it isn't magic. It's possible with a Home Equity Conversion Mortgage (HECM).

Sue's example above illustrates the general concept and application, but for those looking to do more advanced planning with a reverse mortgage, there are many ways to use home equity proactively to enhance financial situations and more efficiently accomplish financial goals.

CONCLUSION

Just like a health check-up, *all* homeowners by age 62 with an existing monthly mortgage balance payment should re-evaluate whether that type of loan is still in their best interest and whether it still fits their plan. For many, the answer is commonly becoming no as they learn of safe alternatives.

Life experience and health concerns often change the idealistic plans we started out with, as they should. It's called wisdom.

Most people's financial lives aren't a straight line. Many people don't actually even have a "plan" they are beholden to. Still more will tell you they ended up in a place they never expected by the time they retired. Because of that, people are leery to work with professionals they fear will judge them or make them feel like a second-class client who doesn't have it all figured out.

While money or individual economic security doesn't buy true happiness, in the world we live in, it does often equate to quality of life, peace of mind, and dignity at a core level. There is no shame in using home equity as part of a full balance sheet approach. In fact, I would say it's the greatest gift you could give yourself as you enter the golden years of life.

A reverse mortgage is the solution many have been looking for, the silver bullet so to speak, but as I've reiterated throughout this book, very few people are properly educated on how reverse mortgages work.

In the past, I've underestimated how much people care what others think of them, even strangers. Reputations and image can be important, but not to the extent it compromises personal and familial integrity. Monte Carlo financial planning success rates have been dropping for clients over the past year—not because they did something wrong, but due to global economic conditions, real systemic geopolitical risks, and muted forecasts. Fluctuation is normal though through economic cycles. What isn't normal is for someone in control of their own finances to keep their head buried in the sand and pretend financial problems will just go away.

Economic conditions are deteriorating and playing out as designed by our Federal Government through the manipulation of money supply and interest rates. Almost every baby boomer started retirement with a 10-plus year bull market run of double-digit portfolio returns. With no change in strategy to accommodate changing economic conditions, many people left on autopilot are destined to prematurely run their portfolios and savings into the ground, giving them fewer housing options in their retirement years.

Talking to my elders over the years, I've learned that one of the ultimate "flexes" a parent can tell their peers is that their kids don't need any of their money. When the opposite is true, it creates a constant cloud over everything the parents spend.

Today, the burden is on each of us to find that equilibrium between living our best overall life and making our money last. When pensions were common, the money you made in your career determined how much you'd live on and your quality of life until you died. But times have changed, and now you must focus on looking forward. Let home equity be the balance sheet equalizer it was meant to be and give yourself the life you worked for all these years.

Somewhere along the way we were programmed that it was normal to leaves hundreds of thousands of dollars to our kids after we've died and have limited control over how it's spent. We measure our love and legacy with a dollar sign. Somehow legacy got turned into an inheritance. Don't get me wrong, I'm totally happy to see money given to children or funding a specific goal for future generations. One of my favorite parts of financial planning was helping discuss trust and estate planning. But a lot of kids are doing okay and would much rather see memories passed on than money. I'd much rather see my mom spend her money to fund a cause she could be active with than pass it to me. Obituaries read a lot better with good stories of what the person was able to accomplish and rarely share how much was left in the bank.

ACKNOWLEDGMENTS

To my many past clients. Having had the benefit of learning life lessons up-close and personal through past clients while I was a young advisor in my 20s, it was impressed upon me early by almost all of them not to make the same mistakes many said they made, focusing too much on work and not enough on the emotional support of their children. Too many past clients told me they'd give up everything they had accumulated to do it over again for better relationships with their kids and grandkids. This impacted me not only personally, but professionally dedicating my career to better life outcomes around me.

In his book *Outliers*, Malcolm Gladwell describes it taking 10,000 hours of intensive practice to achieve mastery of complex skills and materials, so it would not have been possible for me to get the experience needed to put this book together without my past employers. I was fortunate to have many amazing leaders and companies give me the opportunity to put in the 10,000-plus hours of working directly with clients, doing financial planning in the trenches.

To my son, Cole, who has had to listen about reverse mortgages almost every day for well over a year. Setting a positive example and being a good role model to you is what will always power me to keep going.

Finally, to the incredible publishing team at Aloha Publishing, who made this dream come true and helped me find my voice. They had to wrangle me at times as needed, but they put in countless hours, helped organize over 25,000 words of reverse mortgage blogs and journaling I had accumulated over the years behind the scenes, and conducted hours of video interviews over multiple manuscript drafts. This team was professional on every level and I'm forever grateful for their talents.

ABOUT THE AUTHOR

Jason Parker (MBA, CFP®, RICP®) is a reverse mortgage planner and dual channel loan officer supporting homeowners where licensed. He has a finance degree from The Ohio State University, an MBA from Arizona State University, and studied linguistics at the Defense Language Institute in Monterey, CA. He educates eligible homeowners, financial professionals, real estate professionals, and their families on the myriad of incredible benefits and applications of reverse mortgages by teaching classes, conducting seminars, and giving free consultations.

Jason strives to dispel myths and unfair stigmas prohibiting retirees from living their best lives while being candid about the pros and cons given their situations and objectives.

Jason has a formal advanced financial planning background with multiple Fortune 500 companies and building retirement plans for hundreds of families. Throughout his career, he noticed housing and home equity integration planning conversations often weren't going deep enough, leaving clients very underserved on a topic critical to them. This led him down a years-long path studying the reverse mortgage.

Jason served honorably for over seven years (stop-loss) as a non-commissioned officer and paratrooper in the Army Reserve as a

Psychological Operations team chief (Airborne), which included a one-year deployment in Iraq from 2003-2004. For his service, he was awarded a Bronze Star Medal, Purple Heart, Army Commendation Medal, and Combat Action Badge.

In his spare time, Jason enjoys hanging out with his son, coaching youth sports, volunteering with Veterans groups, road trips (checking off national parks), working on his classic car, writing, and open water swimming.

CONNECT WITH ME

- Reverse mortgages just aren't being taught the way they should be in the industry to the professionals that are the ones that need to know the most!
- If you have a client scenario you want to discuss, reach out and we'll walk through it. No obligations, no catch, and you'll walk away feeling better about how reverse mortgages work.

ParkerPlanning.com will always be a domain you can find me at!

ALOHA
PUBLISHING

Made in United States
North Haven, CT
31 October 2024

59674907R00093